THE
OFFICIAL
HIPAA Jungle Map

Your practice's guide to avoiding the HIPAA pitfalls

TODD DIXON

Copyright © 2019 Todd Dixon

All rights reserved. No part of this book may be reproduced, stored, or transmitted by any means—whether auditory, graphic, mechanical, or electronic—without written permission of both the publisher and the author, except in the case of brief excerpts used in critical articles and reviews. Unauthorized reproduction of any part of this work is illegal and is punishable by law.

The Internet is always changing. Some of the links provided in this book, while at the time of writing were accurate, may no longer be available. Where possible, the author has done his best to provide accurate information.

The views in this book are solely those of the author and may not reflect the views of the publisher, and the publisher hereby disclaims any responsibility for them.

Table Of Content

Introduction 1

Part I HIPAA 101 for small practices 5

Introduction to HIPAA 6

Key Parts of HIPAA 18

    The Privacy Rule 18

    The Security Rule 20

    The Breach Notification Rule 22

Why HIPAA is important for small practices 27

Penalties for HIPAA Violations 29

Common misunderstandings about HIPAA 32

    HIPAA isn't mandatory 32

    Using a cloud based EMR means that a practice doesn't have HIPAA responsibilities 34

    Paper based offices don't have to worry about HIPAA 37

    Breach insurance will protect us even if a practice doesn't follow HIPAA regulations 39

    A firewall isn't required under HIPAA regulations 42

    Training isn't required for staff under HIPAA 45

    Business Associate Agreements aren't needed ... 49

    No one goes to jail for violating HIPAA 52

Conclusion 55

Part II Breaches of Protected Health Information 57

Types of breaches and how they occur **58**
    Phishing 61
    Ransomware 71
    Brute Force Attacks 76
    Weak Passwords 83
    Vulnerabilities 95
    Physical Breaches 102
    Employee Breaches 108
    Social Media 113
    Third Party Breaches 118
    Disposing of records 122
    Theft or loss of devices 126
    Websites 131

Part III Your Compliance Plan **136**

Risk Assessment - The Starting Point **138**
    The Risk Assessment is just the starting point 145

Network and Computer Security **149**
    Firewalls 149
    Backups and Disaster Recovery 157
    Server and workstation security 174
    Software Updates 187
    Wireless Security 194
    Mobile Device Security 201

Business Associates **208**

Training **213**

Documentation	218
HIPAA Compliance Road Map	226
Conclusion	234
About the Author	237

INTRODUCTION

HIPAA is one of the most misunderstood pieces of legislation that impacts physicians. Most view it as an unnecessary interference in the way they treat their patients. Part of this comes from the misunderstanding of what HIPAA is actually supposed to do.

HIPAA, as it was enacted and modified over the years, serves two broad purposes. These are:

1. To allow for the portability of patient insurance when they leave one employee to go to another
2. To protect the confidentiality, integrity, and availability of Protected Health Information (PHI) in the possession of Covered Entities and Business Associates

While HIPAA does have power and the potential to cause headaches for practices, it doesn't have to be that way. Most physicians want to do the right thing and protect the data of their patients. HIPAA gives us guidelines on how to

The Official HIPAA Jungle Map

achieve this but also provides for penalties for those who don't want to follow the law.

This book is designed to give you the information you need to get your practice into compliance and then stay compliant.

In Part 1, I will provide a brief overview of what HIPAA really is and how it has been modified over the years. I continue by showing how all of this relates to your practice and the penalties for those that are non-compliant.

In part 2, I discuss what a breach is and the different kinds of breaches under HIPAA law. This covers electronic to paper and everything in between. Where possible, I have supplied actual examples of sites that suffered a breach and what happened to them as a result.

Part 3 builds on what you learned in Part 2 to help you build your own plan to get compliant. One of the common misunderstandings about HIPAA is that compliance is

The Official HIPAA Jungle Map

achieved once and then you are done. I show why that isn't correct and what needs to be done to remain compliant.

HIPAA doesn't have to be a headache or a threat to your practice. If proper planning is done and then followed up with diligence, then it can be managed very well by even the smallest practice. This book will give you the tools to do just that.

Throughout this book, I have added additional information that you may find useful. I have color coded these so that you can easily see what type of information it is.

> News that is related to the section of the book

> Total Geek Out: this is for the geeks who want the WHY of a particular topic

> Training Items: Free training that is related to the topic

This book is not meant to be an exhaustive review of all HIPAA regulations nor should it be considered legal advice. The purpose of this book is help guide you on what your

The Official HIPAA Jungle Map

practice can do to reduce your exposure threats to your protected health information.

Navigating through HIPAA can be like trying to find your way through a dark jungle. This book serves as your map to guide you through the jungle and show you the potential pitfalls you may face.

Let's get started.

Todd Dixon

PART I

HIPAA 101 FOR SMALL PRACTICES

INTRODUCTION TO HIPAA

The Health Insurance Portability and Accountability Act of 1996 (HIPAA) was signed into law by President Bill Clinton on August 21, 1996. It was also known as the Kassebaum–Kennedy Act.

The legislation is composed of five sections and has many purposes. But for the purpose of this book, we will discuss those related to Protected Health Information (PHI). HIPAA created guidelines on how the healthcare industry could use and release PHI. This includes physicians, hospitals, insurance companies, and third-party vendors such as software companies. Standards were created that specified how the data could be used and by whom. At its time of enactment, HIPAA only applied to Covered Entities and was mostly voluntary. This led to a lot of confusion that still lasts today. Many physicians feel that HIPAA is still voluntary and that a breach doesn't need to be reported. However, this is most definitely not the case. HIPAA is mandatory as is reporting breaches.

> **Health Insurance Portability and Accountability Act of 1996**
> # HIPAA
> Its not a suggestion... it's the law!

HITECH

HIPAA was updated in 2009 with the Health Information Technology for Economic and Clinical Health Act (HITECH).

The first major change under HITECH was the Breach Notification Rule. This new rule required organizations to report breaches of PHI directly to the US Department of Health and Human services, to the patients themselves, and to the local news media.

Final Omnibus Rule

In 2013, HIPAA was modified again with the Final Omnibus Rule. This update brought changes to the Security Rule as well as the Breach Notification Rule. The biggest change was including Business Associates under HIPAA regulations. Before that, only Covered Entries were bound to uphold the law.

Another change under the Final Omnibus Rule was a change to the definition of significant harm. Before this new rule, organizations needed proof that significant harm had occurred before reporting a breach but the new rule stated that organizations must now prove that harm did not occur as a result of the breach. This shifted the responsibility back to the Covered Entities and Business Associates.

Covered Entities and Business Associates were required to protect PHI for up to 50 years after a patient's death, a decrease from the indefinite amount before.

New and more severe penalties were introduced with the Final Omnibus Rule.

Common Terms

HIPAA regulations contain a lot of acronyms and terms that can sometimes be confusing. I will list the ones that are the most relevant for you so that it will make things easier to understand as we proceed. These terms will be used many times throughout the book in various ways.

The United States Department of Health and Human Services (HHS)

The office inside the US federal government responsible for enforcing HIPAA regulations. Their sub office, the Office of Civil Rights (OCR) is responsible for investigating breaches or audits. When a breach occurs, Covered Entities are required to report them to this office. This office is also the one that determines civil penalties and fines for breaches.

Protected Health Information (PHI)

Any information that is uniquely identifiable about a patient and their data. HHS has defined 18 separate elements of PHI that must be protected. These are:

1. Patient Names
2. All geographical identifiers smaller than a state
3. Dates (other than year) directly related to the patient

The Official HIPAA Jungle Map

4. Phone Numbers including mobile and work numbers
5. Fax numbers
6. Email addresses
7. Social Security numbers
8. Medical record numbers
9. Health insurance beneficiary numbers
10. Account numbers
11. Certificate/license numbers
12. Vehicle identifiers and serial numbers, including license plate numbers;
13. Device identifiers and serial numbers;
14. Web Uniform Resource Locators (URLs)
15. Internet Protocol (IP) address numbers
16. Biometric identifiers, including finger, retinal and voice prints
17. Full face photographic images and any comparable images
18. Any other unique identifying number, characteristic, or code

The Official HIPAA Jungle Map

Covered Entity

Covered Entities are those that generate healthcare information about patients. These fall into three categories. These are:

Covered Health Care Providers: physicians or providers of healthcare or other medical services or supplies. These entities transmit health information in an electronic format related to transactions that HHS has an established standard. Examples include:

- Chiropractors
- Clinics
- Dentists
- Doctors
- Nursing homes
- Pharmacies
- Psychologists

Health Plans:

- Health insurance companies

- HMOs
- Company Health plans
- Government programs that pay for health care, such as Medicare, Medicaid, and the military and veterans' health care programs

Healthcare Clearinghouse: These are entities that process health information that they receive from another entity and change it into a standardized format. The most common example are electronic data interchange entities that take electronic claims forms and submit them to insurance companies.

Business Associate

Business associates are any person, or third party that work for a Covered Entity that the work involves having to protected health information. Also, anyone that provides services to or for a covered entity in which protected health information would be disclosed.

The Official HIPAA Jungle Map

Examples include:

- Outside billing services
- Third party IT services
- EMR Vendors
- Cloud Storage Providers
- Email Services
- Collection Services
- Attorneys who have access to PHI
- CPA firms who would have access to PHI
- Third party transcriptionists

Employees of a Covered Entity are NOT Business Associates. Contractors performing work for a Covered Entity or Business Associate would be considered Business Associates.

A Business Associate can also have Business Associates. If a third-party billing service were to outsource billing to contractors, they would need to have Business Associate Agreements in place with those contractors.

Privacy Officer

The privacy Officer is the designated person for the Covered Entity or Business Associate that is responsible for the development, implementation, and adherence to the entity's policies concerning PHI. This includes abiding by all federal and state laws.

Security Officer

This role is stipulated in the HIPAA Security Rule. It is the designated person for the Covered Entity or Business Associate that is responsible for creating and implementing policies and procedures that will prevent, detect, contain, and finally, correct breaches of ePHI. The Security Officer is responsible for performing the Risk Assessments.

A single person may serve as both Privacy and Security Officer for a Covered Entity or Business Associate.

Willful neglect

Willful neglect is when an entity makes a conscious choice or intentionally fails to comply with following HIPAA regulations.

Reasonable cause

This is an act or omission in which a Covered Entity or business associate knew, or by exercising reasonable diligence would have known, that the act or omission violated HIPAA regulations. However, in doing so, the Covered Entity or Business Associate did not do so with willful neglect.

Ignorance of the law isn't an excuse and performing an entity's due diligence to protect PHI would have uncovered deficiencies.

Reasonable diligence

This is the business care and prudence that is expected from a person seeking to satisfy a legal requirement under similar circumstances. What would someone else in a similar

The Official HIPAA Jungle Map

situation do to comply with a regulation? Is it reasonable to purchase a hospital level firewall for a single physician office? Likewise, it wouldn't be reasonable for the same single physician office to choose to simply use the router supplied by their Internet vendor.

KEY PARTS OF HIPAA

The Privacy Rule

The Privacy Rule created national standards of protection of the medical records of individuals. The Privacy Rule requires that Covered Entities and Business Associates create appropriate safeguards to protect the privacy of protected health information (PHI). It also establishes exactly what is or is not PHI. The rule sets limits and conditions on how PHI can be used and disclosed. Finally, the Privacy Rule gives rights to patients over their own health information. These rights include the right to obtain and also examine a copy of their health records, and if necessary, to request corrections.

While I did list these in the previous section under Common Terms, I have added them here so that you don't have to go back to reference it.

The Official HIPAA Jungle Map

The 18 parts of PHI are:

1. Patient Names
2. All geographical identifiers smaller than a state
3. Dates (other than year) directly related to the patient
4. Phone Numbers including mobile and work numbers
5. Fax numbers
6. Email addresses
7. Social Security numbers
8. Medical record numbers
9. Health insurance beneficiary numbers
10. Account numbers
11. Certificate/license numbers
12. Vehicle identifiers and serial numbers, including license plate numbers;
13. Device identifiers and serial numbers;
14. Web Uniform Resource Locators (URLs)
15. Internet Protocol (IP) address numbers

16. Biometric identifiers, including finger, retinal and voice prints

17. Full face photographic images and any comparable images

18. Any other unique identifying number, characteristic, or code

The Security Rule

The Security Rule created national standards to protect the electronic protected health information (ePHI) of individuals that is created, received, used, or maintained by a Covered Entity or Business Associate. The Security Rule requires that all Covered Entities and Business Associates create the appropriate administrative, physical and technical safeguards to ensure the confidentiality, integrity, and security of electronic protected health information.

While creating reasonable and appropriate measures for protecting ePHI, entities may use the following to help craft their measure:

- The entity's size, complexity and capabilities
- The technical, hardware and software infrastructure of the entity
- The costs of creating and implementing the security measures
- The likelihood and the possible impact of any risk to the entity's ePHI

A common misunderstanding with these considerations is that an entity may simply opt not to do anything because of budgetary concerns. This is not what the guidelines meant. It meant that a small practice didn't need to purchase the same level of protection that a hospital would need. These guidelines do not relieve an entity of their legal obligations under HIPAA law.

Another area that causes misunderstanding with the Security Rule are the two classes of implementation specifications. These are addressable and required. By the naming convention, it would seem that some items are not required and are therefore, addressable. However, addressable does not mean optional. Addressable means that the organization has some flexibility in how they implement certain controls to achieve the requirement's goal. If you decide not to make use of an addressable requirement, you will need to document why you arrived at this conclusion.

An example would be that I have an addressable goal to obtain a car for my family. It is up to me to decide if I purchase a new car outright, finance it, rent a car, buy a used car, or borrow a car. Whatever I do, the goal is achieved but how I went about achieving that goal was up to me to decide.

The Breach Notification Rule

The Breach Notification Rule requires all HIPAA Covered Entities and Business Associates to report a breach of unsecured protected health information.

What is a breach?

A breach is a disclosure or use of protected health information that is unauthorized. The disclosure would compromise the security or privacy of the PHI. If an unauthorized disclosure has occurred, then it is considered a breach unless the Covered Entity or Business Associate is able to prove that there is a low probability that the PHI was compromised based on a risk assessment. The Risk Assessment must be composed of at least the following:

- What type of PHI was involved and the likelihood that this could be used to identity patients
- Who was the person or persons that performed the unauthorized disclosure and how was the disclosure made?
- Was the PHI actually acquired or viewed?
- The extent to which the risk to the protected health information has been mitigated.

Covered entities and business associates, where applicable, have discretion to provide the required breach notifications following an impermissible use or disclosure without performing a risk assessment to determine the probability that the protected health information has been compromised.

Notification of a breach must be provided to the Department of Health and Human services (HHS) no later than 60 days after discovering the breach. If a breach is less than 500 patient records, then it may be reported annually to HHS.

In addition, Covered Entities are required to notify those individuals that were impacted, or partially impacted, of a breach by letter, within 60 days of the breach discovery. As mentioned above, for breaches of less than 500 patients, reporting to HHS may be delayed until the end of the year but this does not apply to patients impacted by a breach.

All notifications to patients must be made by first class letter and sent to the last known good address. If the patient has given authorization to be contacted via email, notification may be sent via email.

The Official HIPAA Jungle Map

Victims of the breach should be provided with a toll-free number that they can call to get information about the breach.

If the entity has a website, notice of the breach must also be placed on that website of the breach.

A notification must also be made to the media. This is considered a stop gap to ensure that if any patients cannot be contacted due to out of date contact information. This is considered a stop gap measure to ensure notification for any patients that cannot be contacted due to out of date information. This requirement is often overlooked with Covered Entities report breaches.

Business Associates of Covered Entities or other Business Associates are required to notify their upstream entity of a breach that they discover. For example, if an outside billing service was breached, they would be required to report that breach to the Covered Entity who would then be responsible for reporting to HHS. If the same billing service had outsourced an IT service that itself was breached, then then

IT service would be required to report to the billing service, who would in turn, need to report to the Covered Entity.

Under the Breach Notification Rule, there are 3 exceptions of what is considered a breach.

The first exception is if the disclosure or PHI was made in good faith by the employees of a Covered Entity or Business Associate and was in the scope of their approved work.

The second exception applies if someone authorized to access PHI at a Covered Entity or Business Associate discloses information to another employee of the same Covered Entity or Business Associate who is also authorized to access PHI.

The final exception applies if either the Covered Entity or Business Associate believed in good faith that if an unauthorized person received PHI they would not be able to remember the information to make use of it.

WHY HIPAA IS IMPORTANT FOR SMALL PRACTICES

Small practices are bound by HIPAA regulations just as larger practices or hospitals are. However, smaller practices usually have less staff and budget to plan for and execute measures to achieve HIPAA compliance.

While HIPAA regulations do give some leeway to explain these items in your policies and procedures, it is not a license to disregard HIPAA obligations under the law. All Covered Entities and Business Associates are bound by HIPAA regulations. Saying that you didn't have the budget to protect patient data under your obligations will not prevent an audit and fines.

Attackers also know that small offices are less likely to be prepared so they focus more on those. This is considered low hanging fruit as an attacker can get access to a large number of patient records without a lot of work invested. In addition, staff are less likely to have been trained or kept up to date on the newest threats to patient privacy. Smaller practices are less likely to update their hardware and software to stay current and protected along with having their networks monitored for compliance and attacks.

Because of all of these, the small practice has a higher risk potential than other entities. The good news is that it doesn't have to be expensive for a small practice to adhere to HIPAA regulations and protect patient data.

PENALTIES FOR HIPAA VIOLATIONS

Violators of HIPAA regulations can be subjected financial penalties, and in some cases, jail time. These penalties are broken down into 4 categories.

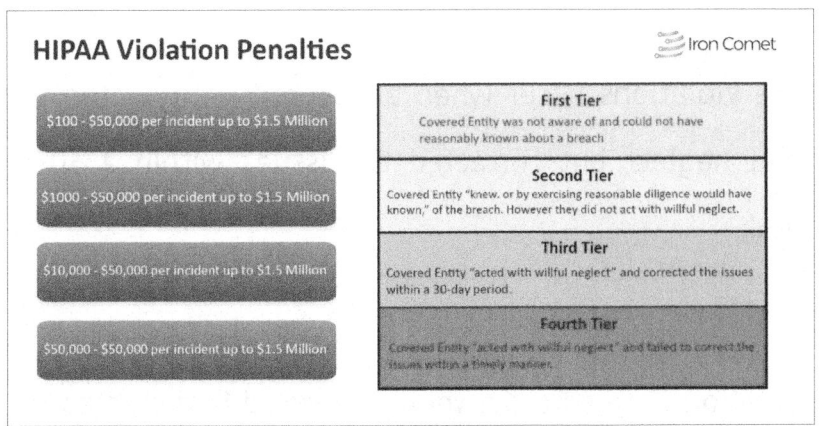

Civil Penalties

Tier 1

In this tier, the Covered Entity was not aware and could not have reasonably known about a breach that occurred. In these cases, the fines are from $100 up to $50,000 per incident, with a maximum penalty of $1.5 million.

The Official HIPAA Jungle Map

Tier 2

These violations occur when a Covered Entity knew or if they had exercised reasonable judgment, would have known that a breach occurred. However, they did not act with willful neglect. That is an important distinction.

Tier 3

These violations occur when a Covered Entity acted with willful neglect but corrected the issues within a 30-day period.

Tier 4

A violation in this tier is when a Covered Entity acted with willful neglect and failed to correct the issues in a timely manner. This is the worst level of HIPAA violation and can result in much harsher penalties and corrective action programs. This is reserved for those entities that really tried not to follow their obligation under the law.

Criminal Penalties

When criminal penalties are levied, they are handled by the US Department of Justice. Covered entities and specified individuals, as explained below, who "knowingly" obtain or disclose individually identifiable health information, in violation of the Administrative Simplification Regulations, face a fine of up to $50,000, as well as imprisonment up to 1 year.

Offenses committed under false pretenses allow penalties to be increased to a $100,000 fine, with up to 5 years in prison.

Finally, offenses committed with the intent to sell, transfer or use individually identifiable health information for commercial advantage, personal gain or malicious harm permit fines of $250,000 and imprisonment up to 10 years.

COMMON MISUNDERSTANDINGS ABOUT HIPAA

In this next section I will cover some of the more common misunderstandings that surround how HIPAA works in relation to small practices. With each misunderstanding, I have provided an actual case where it will illustrate what happened with an entity who had the same misunderstanding.

HIPAA isn't mandatory

This is the most common misconception about HIPAA – maybe because at one time, it was true.

When HIPAA was first introduced, it was voluntary. However, starting in 2003, compliance with the HIPAA Privacy Rule became mandatory. In 2006, compliance with the HIPAA Security Rule also became mandatory.

The Official HIPAA Jungle Map

Starting in 2008, the Department of Health and Human Services Office of Civil Rights began to enforce fines against sites found to be in non-compliance. Each year, the total amount of fines has increased as OCR increases their investigations.

Year	Total Fines
2008	$100,000
2009	$2,250,000
2010	$1,035,000
2011	$6,165,500
2012	$4,700,000
2013	$4,400,000
2014	$7,500,000
2015	$6,193,000
2016	$23,504,800
2017	$20,393,200
2018	$28,683,400

Another reason that compliance is sometimes thought to be voluntary is that some of the items in the HIPAA Security Rule are Addressable. Addressable, however, doesn't mean optional. Addressable means you have some discretion about how you resolve that item.

HIPAA is not optional. It is mandatory for any Covered Entity or Business Associate.

Using a cloud based EMR means that a practice doesn't have HIPAA responsibilities

Many practices think that if they use an Internet based EMR product, also called cloud based, that they no longer need to worry about HIPAA. The theory is that all PHI is now on the servers of the EMR company rather than on any computers in the practice.

Unfortunately, this is a very dangerous and expensive belief to have.

HIPAA isn't only the data stored in an EMR. It is also how your practice interacts with patients. Perhaps an employee

The Official HIPAA Jungle Map

sent a fax that was supposed to go to your billing company to another company instead. It contained all patients that the practice saw that day. That is now a breach because the PHI went to another party that wasn't authorized to see it. This has nothing to do with the EMR data.

In addition, ePHI is on every computer in a typical practice. If you were to look at the documents folder of any workstation, you would likely find patient data. In addition, when documents are scanned, they may be uploaded to a cloud based EMR, but the original document is still on the computer. Faxes are also handled in a similar manner. Whether you use a fax server or paper faxes, those documents reside in your practice.

Is your practice completely paperless? Including intake forms, patient records from other providers, and other forms of communications? Do you have business associate agreements in place with your vendors? What about with your EMR provider?

The Official HIPAA Jungle Map

A cloud based EMR doesn't remove the Risk Assessment or training requirements of HIPAA. Staff must be trained on the threats that exist to PHI.

> **The cloud doesn't exisit.**
> Your data is on someone else's computer

An example of this is the case of Peachtree Orthopedic in Georgia. This practice used a cloud based EMR that itself wasn't breached. The practice was attacked by a hacker group called the Dark Overlord. The hackers used phishing emails to infect computers on the network. From there, the hackers were able to steal the data of over 500,000 patients. Remember, this is a cloud based EMR and the hackers were still able to steal all of the data.

The EMR vendor wasn't breached because the hackers had stolen the login information from the practice itself.

Peachtree Orthopedic notified HHS about the breach and then also notified their patients.

You can read about this breach here:

https://www.wsbtv.com/news/local/atlanta/peachtree-orthopedics-data-breach-put-thousands-at-risk/475682805

Paper based offices don't have to worry about HIPAA

HIPAA isn't just about electronic protected health information (ePHI). It concerns all patient records in whatever format they may be in. This can be paper charts, billing statements, faxes, phone messages or even dictations.

Patient information exists in every practice whether they used computers or not. Computers make it easy to protect data but it also makes it easy to steal large amounts of data at once. With paper charts, for someone to steal 10,000 records would take a lot of effort.

The Official HIPAA Jungle Map

Before hacking attacks and phishing threats, improper disposal of records was one of the most common items to generate fines. It usually involved entities throwing away paper charts without shredding them first. Paper charts take up a lot of space and it's easy to throw them away thinking that the trash makes them safe. When records are no longer needed, they must be disposed of in a secure manner that prevents them from falling into the hands of others.

Cornell Pharmacy of Denver Colorado paid a fine of $125,000 for improperly disposing of patient records. In 2012, the pharmacy threw away the records of 1,610 patients in a dumpster that was accessible to the public. This resulted in a HIPAA breach.

You can read about this breach here –

http://www.hhs.gov/ocr/privacy/hipaa/enforcement/examples/cornell/cornell-cap.pdf

The Official HIPAA Jungle Map

Breach insurance will protect us even if a practice doesn't follow HIPAA regulations

We are all accustomed to thinking insurance is there to protect us in the event of unforeseen events. Examples include flood and earthquake insurance. We hope we don't need them but are happy we have them when they are needed.

The Official HIPAA Jungle Map

A new type of insurance is available to protect data: cybersecurity insurance. Many believe that this is all they need to protect them. Why go to the expense of complying with HIPAA when you can just get insurance in case a breach ever happens right? After all, that is what insurance is for.

Insurance policies require that we all do our part as well. For example, if your car had failing brakes that hadn't been maintained in years and you had a car accident, do you think insurance would protect you? You failed to keep the car in a safe condition and contributed to the accident.

This is also true for cybersecurity insurance. All cybersecurity insurance policies require that the entity they are protecting perform their due diligence. You couldn't leave the doors of your house wide open and unlocked and then complain about a burglar. Cybersecurity insurance requires a Risk Assessment be performed and each item that is uncovered, be addressed. Failing to do so or performing security under common best practices like the NIST framework would be grounds for the claim to be denied.

The Official HIPAA Jungle Map

Each policy has its own requirements in the application for what an entity does to protect data.

Cottage Health System had a breach where they hired a third-party IT company to install a new server. The server was improperly installed and allowed access to 32,000 patient records online. The IT company didn't have its own insurance and couldn't defend itself in the resulting lawsuit. Cottage Health relied upon its own insurance policy from Columbia Casualty. Columbia Casualty provided legal representation to Cottage and settled the lawsuit for $4.1 million.

However, afterwards, Columbia Casualty performed their own investigation. They discovered that what Cottage Healthcare claimed on the insurance application about how protected data and what they actually did in their practice didn't match. They in turn, sued Cottage Healthcare for $4.1 million for failing to adhere to the contract.

Even worse for the practice, Columbia stated that failing to do the basic steps to secure the data allowed the breach to happen in the first place. Insurance won't protect you if you don't do your part.

You can read about this here –

https://www.law360.com/cases/5859bd989c28062a5c000416

A firewall isn't required under HIPAA regulations

This one is a bit tricky because the word firewall never appears in any HIPAA regulations. These regulations were written to be technology neutral: they don't go into a lot of specifics on how to do things. However, they do specify performing best efforts and best practices. The NIST framework is the most common best practice for cyber security in the industry and what most of HIPAA is built on.

If your practice is connected to the Internet in any way, even if you are using a cloud based EMR, you must have a firewall.

A firewall is a device that separates one network from another. In the case of practices, it separates their internal, private network from the Internet. Firewalls are the gatekeeper of all data traffic coming in and leaving your practice. Modern firewall devices are called Unified Threat Managers because they sit at this point. These devices can inspect traffic looking for malicious items such as malware and ransomware. They can also filter spam and monitor for intrusions.

The Official HIPAA Jungle Map

Another common misunderstanding is that the device supplied by your internet company is a firewall or that the consumer grade wireless routers are sufficient. These devices may even advertise themselves as having firewalls built in. However, nearly every consumer grade router has been found to have numerous bugs that allow hackers to take them over. In addition, vendors rarely release updates to block these holes and even if they do, consumers don't install them. Using one of these devices is basically the same as not having a firewall and won't protect you from breaches of your PHI.

However, having a firewall alone isn't enough. It must be monitored. This means someone is watching the firewall logs for events or signs of intrusion. Not monitoring the logs is like having an alarm system that doesn't call the police when a burglar breaks in. It's pretty useless.

If you are thinking because HIPAA doesn't specify a firewall is protection for your practice, consider the case of Idaho State University. The university had installed a firewall but left inactive for a period of 10 months. In effect, they had no firewall. A breach of 17,500 patient records occurred during the time the firewall wasn't activated. The breach was found and reported to OCR. OCR's investigation found that the Idaho State had not adequately protected patient data because they were not using or monitoring a firewall.

OCR assessed a fine of $400,000 for not having and monitoring a firewall.

You can read more about this breach and resolution here:

https://www.hhs.gov/hipaa/for-professionals/compliance-enforcement/agreements/idaho-state-university/index.html

Training isn't required for staff under HIPAA

This HIPAA myth is either that training isn't necessary or that training once per year from a set videos is sufficient. The purpose of training isn't to check a box on your practice's HIPAA compliance. The purpose of training is to make sure that staff is aware of the threats that are possible to your practice's PHI. Because threats are always emerging, once per year training won't work. In addition, your training should include your practice's policies and procedures on how to handle PHI and breaches. That can't be learned watching a video series.

Training is mandatory under HIPAA regulations. This can be found in two places: as an Administrative Requirement of the HIPAA Privacy Rule (45 CFR §164.530) and an Administrative Safeguard of the HIPAA Security Rule (45 CFR §164.308).

The one specific guideline given for both Covered Entities and Business Associates is:

"implement a security awareness and training program for all members of the workforce"

Notice that is says a program for all members. This would indicate it's not a single event and since its security awareness, it must be ongoing as security threats are always changing. Five years ago, we didn't have the threat of ransomware, but now it is a very real threat to practices. Phishing has now emerged as one of the greatest threats to the security of PHI. Has your staff been specifically trained on how to spot a phishing email attack?

In addition, recently HHS came up with a standard for how much effort an entity put into their compliance program. While not focused on training, it does address the quality of training.

Please notice rating 4.

"Evidence of training is poorly documented and generic."

This means that standardized training isn't acceptable for compliance.

The Official HIPAA Jungle Map

Rating	Description
1	The audit results indicate the entity is in compliance with both goals and objectives of the selected standards and implementation specifications.
2	The audit results indicate that the entity substantially meets criteria; it maintains appropriate policies and procedures, and documentation and other evidence of implementation meet requirements.
3	Audit results indicate entity efforts minimally address audited requirements; analysis indicates that entity has made attempts to comply, but the implementation is inadequate, or some efforts indicate a misunderstanding of requirements.
4	Audit results indicate the entity made negligible efforts to comply with the audited requirements - e.g. policies and procedures submitted for review are copied directly from an association template; evidence of training is poorly documented and generic.
5	The entity did not provide OCR with evidence of serious attempt to comply with the Rules and enable individual rights with regard to PHI.

Phishing attacks are a good example of why training can't be generic and must be timely and up to date with the current threats to PHI.

An example of this is the case of Peachtree Orthopedic in Georgia that I cited above. The practice was attacked by a hacker group called the Dark Overlord. The hackers used phishing emails to infect computers on the network. From there, the hackers were able to steal the data of over 500,000 patients.

I used this example for training as well to illustrate how proper training could have prevented a phishing attack from occurring at this practice.

One of the items in any corrective action program for a breach of this nature is training. Training for staff on how to handle phishing attacks, training to handle breaches, etc.

You can read about this breach here:

https://www.wsbtv.com/news/local/atlanta/peachtree-orthopedics-data-breach-put-thousands-at-risk/475682805

Business Associate Agreements aren't needed

Most Covered Entities understand that they need Business Associate Agreements. The confusion often happens when they try to determine who needs the agreement. In addition, many Business Associates themselves aren't aware that they need to sign them. Many will refuse to sign the document saying that it doesn't apply to them.

The Official HIPAA Jungle Map

Another point of confusion is that many Business Associates themselves need to have Business Associate Agreements with their own vendors. An example would be a third-party biller that has contractors working for them. Those contractors would need to sign Business Associate Agreements for the billing service.

For a Covered Entity, any outside person or service who has regular access to your PHI requires a Business Associate Agreement to be signed. These agreements should be kept in your HIPAA documentation. If changes are made over time, a new agreement would be needed.

Here is an example of a site that was fined for not having Business Associate Agreements in place.

Advanced Care Hospitalists PL (ACH) engaged a third party to perform services for them between November 2011 and June 2012. This third party was an individual that represented himself as being a representative of a Florida-based company named Doctor's First Choice Billing, Inc. This individual provided medical billing services to ACH under the name of Doctor's First Choice Billing, Inc. One issue is that Doctor's First Choice Billing, Inc. claims to have no knowledge of this arraignment or even the individual claiming to represent them.

A local hospital noticed in February 2014 that patient data for ACH was visible on the website belonging to Doctor's First Choice Billing, Inc. After investigation, it was discovered that 8,855 patients were affected in the breach. ACH filed a breach notification.

OCR began their investigation and discovered that ACH never had a Business Associate Agreement in place with individual or Doctor's First Choice Billing, Inc. The investigation also revealed that even though ACH had been in operation since 2005, it did not conduct a Risk Assessment until 2014.

OCR fined ACH $500,000 and required them to imitate a corrective action plan that would include the use of a Business Associate Agreement with all third parties had access to ACH's PHI. The plan also required that ACH perform an enterprise wide Risk Assessment and implement policies and procedures to bring them into compliance with the HIPAA Privacy Rule.

You can read the press statement here:

https://www.hhs.gov/hipaa/for-professionals/compliance-enforcement/agreements/ach/index.html

No one goes to jail for violating HIPAA

HIPAA regulations, while laws, aren't usually prosecuted as crimes. Most HIPAA investigations are handled with civil penalties by HHS OCR. However, when a case needs to be prosecuted for criminal wrongdoing, the case is referred to the Department of Justice. In addition, States are free to build and prosecute their own cases for violations.

Criminal cases for HIPAA are not common, that is true. But it does happen and it's not always for the violations you might think. Sometimes they are the cases of large amounts of data stolen or data used for personal gain. But usually they are for much smaller infractions.

The Official HIPAA Jungle Map

In 2010, Huping Zhou became the first person in the United states to be sent to prison for violating HIPAA laws. What could have been so bad that it necessitated jailtime? He must have stolen and sold patient data or released celebrity information to the tabloids, right? Not quite.

Mr. Zhou was a cardiologist in his native China but while working to pass exams for the United States, he worked as a researcher at UCLA Health System in California. In 2003, he received notice that UCLA was terminating his employment. However, that same day, Mr. Zhou accessed the medical records of his immediate supervisor and other coworkers.

Over a period of three weeks, he viewed the medical records of thousands of patients including high profile celebrities such as Drew Barrymore, Arnold Schwarzenegger, Tom Hanks, and Leonardo DiCaprio.

Mr. Zhou never disclosed any of the information he found, even to his wife. He didn't sell it or make use of it in any way. He simply viewed it. However, he didn't have a

The Official HIPAA Jungle Map

medically necessary reason for doing so. HIPAA doesn't allow for the viewing of patient records by anyone that doesn't have a medical need to do so.

He was charged with four misdemeanor counts of accessing and reading the confidential medical records. He was later sentenced to four months in federal prison for the violations.

If you would like to read more about this case, please go to:

https://journal.ahima.org/2010/04/29/californian-sentenced-to-prison-for-hipaa-violation/

CONCLUSION

Due to the misunderstandings surrounding HIPAA regulations, a lot of myths have developed. Part of this is also due to the amount of misinformation that is available online about HIPAA. Companies offering HIPAA certification or compliance are abundant. But no one can make you HIPAA compliant. Only you can do that for your own practice.

But make no mistake, HIPAA is real and enforcement is common. It can be very costly for practices to just assume they "have it covered" or stick their head in the sand. HIPAA compliance isn't negotiable.

The Official HIPAA Jungle Map

Dr. Bird's default response when he hear's the words HIPAA compliance. Don't be like Dr. Bird. HIPAA compliance isn't negotiable.

PART II

BREACHES OF PROTECTED HEALTH INFORMATION

TYPES OF BREACHES AND HOW THEY OCCUR

A breach is a release of Protected Health Information to someone who is not authorized to have access to it. This is a very broad definition that covers a wide range of situations. Also, not all breaches are malicious as they are completely unintentional. HIPAA regulations have rules for all of these.

In this section, I will discuss the different kinds of breaches and how they can threaten your practice. In addition, I will show how each breach occurs and what you can do to protect against each one.

FULL DISCLOSURE: This in no way covers every conceivable type of breach. The ones in this book are the most common that you are likely to face. Your situation may be different and a thorough Risk Assessment will reveal what types of breaches you are most likely to face.

The Official HIPAA Jungle Map

For example, if your practice doesn't use email, then phishing attacks, though extremely common, are not a threat to you. This is why all things HIPAA begin with the Risk Assessment. Your Risk Assessment will outline the threats that you are most likely to face and how you can reduce the risk that they pose to your practice.

This section of the book will divide breaches into two broad categories: electronic and non-electronic. From there, I will further break those down into types of breaches that occur under each. With each, I will give examples of how they can occur and what you can do to protect your practice against them.

Some of these can be technical in nature and I work hard to strip away any unnecessary geek speak. That is often why a lot of these issues don't get addressed in practices. It can be very intimidating for non-technical people to work with these threats. The goal of this section is to help you have a good understanding of how these threats can cause breaches in your practice and what you can do to prevent them.

SECURITY BREACH

Electronic Data Breach

As we move more and more to Electronic Health Records (EHR), the more patient data is available on computers. When charts were on paper, it would have been difficult for a thief to get more than a few charts at one time. Imagine a thief stealing one hundred thousand charts of paper. But with charts now in electronic format, it has become easy to steal enormous amounts of patient data quickly. The convenience of medical records has also opened up new avenues for attacks.

In this section, I will detail many of the more common ways that electronic data can be breached and stolen. With each threat, I give an explanation of what it is, how it threatens your practice, an example, and finally, a way to defend your practice from it. These attacks can range from email phishing attacks to hacking attacks and everything in between.

Phishing

Phishing is when an attacker sends an email that appears to be legitimate to a user but it isn't. The purpose of the email is to get the user to perform an action they normally wouldn't do such as installing malicious software or clicking on a link. Attackers use phishing emails to get users to enter in personal information on fake websites that are made to look identical to legitimate banking or credit card sites. The user would enter their username and password into the site and be redirected to the real bank site afterwards. Now the attacker has collected that user's bank login information.

Another reason attackers use phishing emails is to get the user to click on an attachment such as a PDF or Microsoft Word Document. The document is actually infected with malware that would give the attacker remote access to the user's computer.

Detecting phishing emails can be difficult because most of them prey on our fears or curiosity. Email can seem to be from UPS updating the user on the status of a delivery or from a bank updating on a large withdrawal from the person's account. These emails are sent out to hundreds of thousands of people at the same time so the likelihood that a few have a package being delivered at that time or bank with the bank in the email, is quite high.

Another common tactic is around tax season to make the emails appear to come from the Internal Revenue Service (IRS). It may threaten that an impending levy is coming if

The Official HIPAA Jungle Map

the user doesn't act now. The IRS NEVER emails taxpayers. They will send paper letters.

Examples of phishing emails

Here are some examples of phishing emails I have received. Some are very good and take a bit of time to detect. However, others are very poor attempts by an attacker to gain access to a system. There are 4 examples below that illustrate the psychology of the attacks. 2 emails pretend to be from UPS (United Parcel Service), one is from Bank of America, and the last is from JP Morgan Chase bank.

Let's get started.

Bankofamerica Business

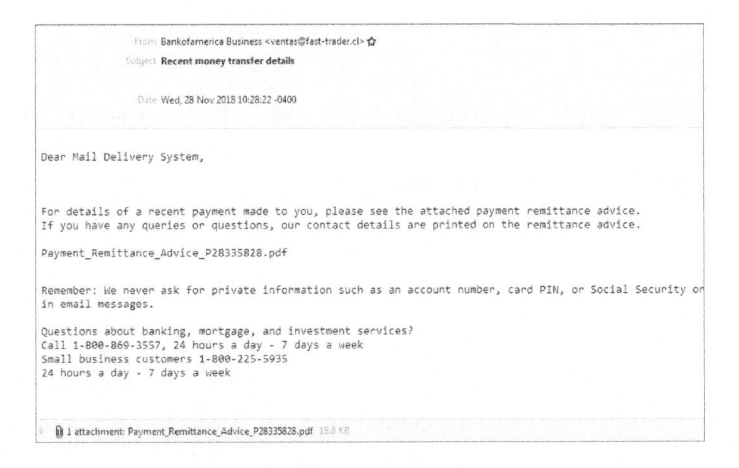

Bankofamerica phishing email attempt

The Official HIPAA Jungle Map

Sometimes detecting phishing emails isn't hard, like this very poor attempt to be from Bank of America.

This email pretends to be from Bank of America. However, they misspell it to be Bankofamerica Business. That is the first red flag. The email references a remittance advice that is included as an attachment. The attachment is PDF file. However, the file is infected. Upon clicking it, the computer would become infected with malware.

The second red flag is the from address for the email. The label says Bankofamerican Business but the actual address is ventas@fast-trader.cl – not a valid Bank of America address.

The email tries to assure you that they never ask for personal information via email.

UPS Phishing Email 1

> From: UPS Quantum View <careers@kichton.com>
> Subject: UPS Ship Notification, Tracking Number 8TDA67332589213391
> Date: Mon, 03 Dec 2018 22:00:01 +0530
> Return-Path: <careers@kichton.com>
>
> **The status of your package has changed.**
>
> **Exception Reason:** A transportation accident has delayed delivery.
> **Exception Resolution:** We've missed the scheduled transfer time. This may cause a delay.
>
> ---
>
> Scheduled Delivery Date: **Monday, 12/03/2018**
>
> UPS shipment tracking
>
> ---
>
> Tracking Number: 8TDA67332589213391
> From: **Amazon**
>
> Thank you for your business.
>
> 📎 1 attachment: Number - 8TDA67332589213391.doc 131 KB

UPS Phishing attempt email 1

This email pretends to be from UPS Quantum View. This is the correct name for UPS' tracking system. But notice that the actual email address is careers@kichton.com – this isn't UPS. The email is trying to scare the user that their package has been delayed. If you were expecting a package at that time, you would might open the attachment without thinking too much about it. The email also indicates the package is from Amazon. This is a likely source for many people for packages.

This email also contains an attachment to get the user to open. This Microsoft Word document contains the infected payload. The payload is the malicious software that activates when the user clicks on it.

UPS phishing email #2

```
From: UPS <bp@360businesssolution.net>
Subject: UPS Schedule Delivery Update, Tracking Number 7EOZ14175532604180
Date: Wed, 06 Jun 2018 15:36:18 +0400
Return-Path: <bp@360businesssolution.net>
```

The status of your package has changed.

Exception Reason: A transportation accident has delayed delivery.
Exception Resolution: We've missed the scheduled transfer time. This may cause a delay.

Scheduled Delivery Date: **Wednesday, 06/06/2018**

Shipment Details

Shipment number: 7EOZ14175532604180
From: **Nick Chuang**
Number of Packages: 2
Scheduled Delivery: 06/06/2018
Weight: 18.1 KGS

UPS phishing attempt #2

This is the second UPS email. It also has a bogus from address bp@360businessolution.net) but the reason I included it is that it doesn't use an attachment. This email has a malicious link in it. It is the shipment number (usually referred to as the tracking number). Clicking on this number takes the user to a bogus site that attempts to harvest user information. The weight is also listed in kilograms, which in the United States, would be abnormal. If you're in the US and see this, that is another red flag.

JP Morgan Chase

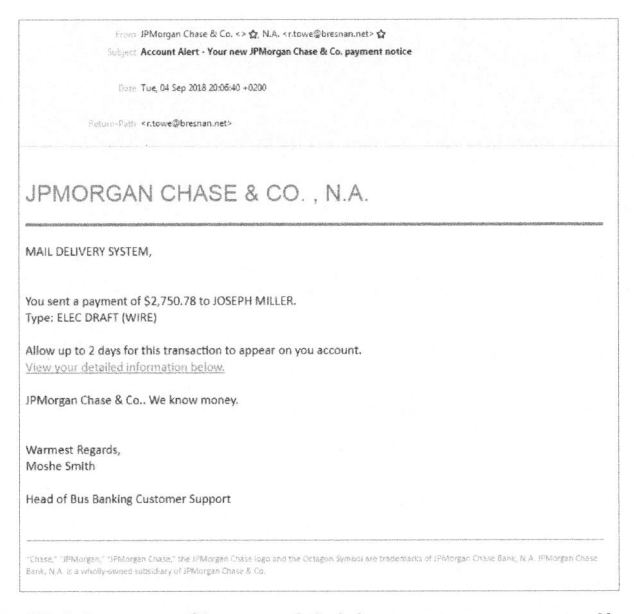

JP Morgan Chase phishing attempt email

The Official HIPAA Jungle Map

Our final example is from JP Morgan Chase bank. This one preys on your fear that a wire transfer in the amount of $2,750.78 has been withdrawn from your account. It was sent to a Joseph Miller. This is a small enough amount not to be considered outlandish. That way, most people will likely freak out and assume this is some mistake and click the supplied link. Like the UPS email above, this email link goes to a bogus site that will attempt to capture personal information from the user.

The email's return address is r.towe@bresnan.net – this is not a valid JP Morgan email address.

These examples show how phishing can look to a victim. These are pretty easy to understand and detecting them as phishing is not difficult. However, some phishing emails come looking nearly identical to the real thing. How are users supposed to know the difference?

How can you protect yourself from phishing attacks?

To defend yourself against phishing email attacks, there is no silver bullet. Protection is done in layers with each layer reinforcing the other to provide protection.

Your first layer is training your staff. Create a program that helps all staff be able to identify phishing email that they may receive. In addition, training should include the potential consequences of falling for this form of attack. While some phishing emails are very sophisticated and difficult to detect, most are not.

> **Free phishing training?**
>
> Phishing has become such a problem that Google has created a quiz that teaches users how to spot fake email. It is a good resource to add to your practice's training program. You can find it at:
>
> https://phishingquiz.withgoogle.com/

The next layer of defense is to make sure each computer on your network is using a commercial anti-malware program. In the past, these were called anti-virus programs. But the threats have evolved and so has the defensive software. Examples include Webroot (www.webroot.com), Malwarebytes (www.malwarebytes.com), and Emsisoft (www.emsisoft.com). Be sure to use the full, commercial version of whatever software you do choose. The full versions offer real time scanning and protection. This means that while you are surfing or viewing emails, the software is watching for signs of malware. If you use free versions of these programs, you won't get this protection.

The final layer of defense is email and DNS filtering performed by your firewall or Unified Threat Manager (UTM). Many of these attacks can be stopped simply by filtering spam. However, the more sophisticated attacks will still be able to slip through. This is where DNS filtering comes in. DNS filters that are connected to blocking lists are usually updated many times per day. These lists have all the newly found domains that are being used for malicious attacks. If your firewall is configured to use them, then if a user clicks on a link in a phishing email that is contained in these databases, the user will be prevented from visiting the site.

Another option is to use DNS filtering services such as 1.1.1.1 (https://1.1.1.1/) and Quad9 (www.quad9.com). These are both free and can help protect your network from users accidently clicking on links that they shouldn't be.

Ransomware

Ransomware is malicious software that invades a computer and begins to encrypt all of the data it finds on the computer. It is careful to leave the operating system alone as it targets your documents, pictures, and data for programs like QuickBooks. Some ransomware is able to move across your network and perform the same attack on each computer on the network.

Once your data is encrypted, the ransomware will show you a warning telling you that all of your data has been encrypted and offering to give you the password to decrypt it all for a fee.

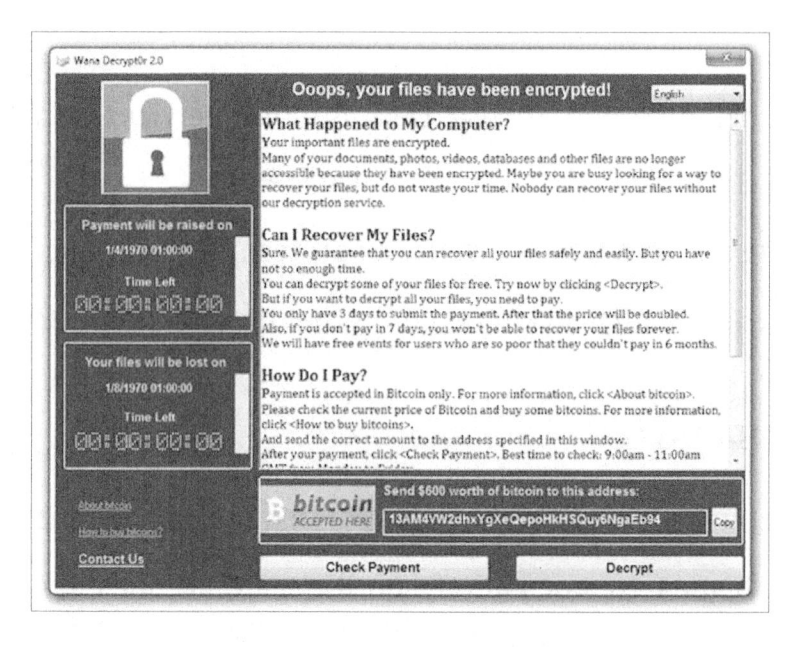

Example of ransomware

In other words, your data is being held ransom until you pay up.

Payment is handled via Bitcoin, a semi-anonymous online money that can be sent anywhere in the world. This helps attackers to work from the safety of other countries with little threat that they will be caught or punished.

For the criminal, the end result is low risk but high reward. How high is the reward?

> **Jackson County pays $400,000 ransom to attackers**
>
> In March of 2019, the computer network for all of Jackson County, Georgia became infected with a ransomware strain known as Ryuk. This was created by a shadowy cybercriminal gang operating out of Eastern Europe. This group is focused on healthcare and local governments because they know that these are usually easier targets that will pay the ransoms.
>
> In the case of Jackson County, most of the county's IT systems were affected. The FBI was notified and a cybersecurity firm was called in. The firm negotiated with the attackers for a payment of $400,000. After the

> payment was made, the county received the decryption key and began to decrypt their network.
>
> The end result for the criminal gang? A Low risk as they are unlikely to be found or extradited, with a high reward of $400,000.

Why are HIPAA ransomware attacks worse than attacks for other businesses?

Most businesses in the United States aren't under compliance regulations such as HIPAA. HIPAA requires Covered Entities and Business Associates to actively protect the data in their control. There (are?) strict penalties for those who do not comply and are breached. This means that sites that become infected are faced with not only the ransom itself, but also the potential for federal fines and also lawsuits by patients. HIPAA ransomware attacks have the potential to be far worse and the overall cost to physicians is much higher.

Because of this, attackers target the healthcare industry. They know that sites must be back up and running as quickly as possible and also have HIPAA regulations to contend with. This increases the chances of the ransom being paid. Many of those infected may also want to keep it quiet so that they can avoid reporting the breach. However, this usually doesn't work out well.

Those that choose to not pay the ransom often have enormous expenses to pay for the cleanup. The city of Atlanta chose not to pay a ransom of $51,000 and instead have run up a bill of over $17 million.

https://www.ajc.com/news/confidential-report-atlanta-cyber-attack-could-hit-million/GAljmndAF3EQdVWlMcXS0K/

According to the McAfee Threat Report for June 2018, healthcare saw a 47% rise in ransomware in the beginning of 2018. This was partially due to the SamSam ransomware. You can read that report at:

https://www.mcafee.com/enterprise/en-us/assets/reports/rp-quarterly-threats-jun-2018.pdf

According to Datto, ransomware costs businesses worldwide, $75 Billion per year. This cost reflects ransoms paid, cleanup and patching of infected systems. Each year the amount grows as the profitability increases for the attackers: low risk, high reward. Until it doesn't make money for them, they will continue to use this tactic.

Brute Force Attacks

A brute force attack is when an attacker attempts many passwords with the goal of eventually guessing the correct password. The attack will go through every possible password until the right one is found. It is one of least effective attack methods as it takes a lot of time and resources. However, if enough time is taken and the target doesn't have defenses in place, eventually the correct password will be found.

The Official HIPAA Jungle Map

The best way to think of brute force attacks is to think about a thief with a box of keys. He will try each key until he finds the right one for your house. But once he has it, he as complete access to your house.

To make the attack more efficient, attackers want to use guesses that are more likely to yield the correct answer. For this, an attacker uses a list of passwords called a dictionary, a long list of passwords that the attacker will feed into the brute force program.

An example would look like this –

123456   111111

password   1234567

123456789   sunshine

12345678   qwerty

12345   iloveyou

These are the 10 most commonly used passwords. The brute force program would send all of these passwords to the target, trying one after the other.

Attackers can download dictionary files from the Internet or create a custom dictionary. These files are created by attackers but also by security researchers for legitimate purposes such as penetration testing.

When sites are breached, their password files are often dumped online. Hackers and security researchers alike will compile dictionaries using these files because these are actual passwords that users have used. This makes them very valuable since most people use similar passwords. This is why secure passwords are the best defense against brute force attacks. If the amount of time it would take to guess the password is prohibitively long, the attacker will move onto another method of attack.

Programs that generate dictionaries can also customize them by adding numbers automatically to the end of the password list, change common characters like S to $, and randomly capitalize letters. This means that using a password like sunshine above, but changing it to $unSh1ne would not make it secure.

How does this impact small medical practices?

One of the common ways for practices to allow for remote access is using Microsoft's Remote Desktop or Terminal Services. This setup is often used to allow remote billers or physicians to have access to the network. When set up improperly, the server is directly on the Internet without protection and the attacker is able to brute force the user name and password. Over time, the password will be cracked and the attacker will have access to the server using that compromised account. This is especially common when the proper controls have not been configured on the server and there is no monitoring being performed to alert the practice to the attack. This sort of attack is very common for ransomware cybercriminals. After breaking into a network via password guessing on a remote desktop server, they will begin to infect that computer with the ransomware. For the attacker, this is a low risk way to break into a network because most practices aren't aware that it's happening. The first indication of the attack is when the site sees the ransomware popup on a computer.

The other common way this can damage a small practice is when an attacker focuses on an email account or web account. These can often be brute forced and will give the attacker access. If a practice is sending PHI via email without encryption, itself already a breach, now the attacker has access to this data.

The Official HIPAA Jungle Map

Another area where brute force attacks can be used is in an offline mode. This means that the attacker was able to capture password hashes. Password hashes are an encrypted version of the password. The attacker doesn't have the actual password, just the hash. They will run the cracking program against these hashes using dictionaries on their own computer. The attack doesn't take place across the internet and therefore cannot be detected. All the work is being done on the attacker's computer. This is very common in wireless password cracking. The attacker will listen to, or sniff, wireless traffic at a target. Although the traffic is encrypted, the attacker can still see that data, they just can't read it. After enough traffic has been captured, the attacker will have a hash of the password used to secure the wireless network. Keep in mind, that this doesn't mean the attacker can access the wireless network yet. When back at their home location, the attacker will run brute force programs against this hash until it cracks the password. This is an entirely passive attack and undetectable by the victim.

The Official HIPAA Jungle Map

Later, the attacker can return to the target and use the now decrypted wireless password to access the wireless network just as if they were inside the building.

Wireless passwords can be up to 63 characters long but most people choose short and easy to remember passwords. No one wants to type in

$8g9cnfDa7@hbPke&ga1@=j8ZALF$*#&5^68GBbDA1Rjfd

each time that they need to add a new device to a wireless network. It's much easier to type in sunshine1 instead. However, this convenience trades security and makes the network very easy to break into.

With modern cracking tools, wireless networks are laughably easy to break into, on most occasions.

Brute force isn't the best method of breaking into a target but since most people choose weak passwords for all of the important items, brute force is a useful tool for attackers.

Weak Passwords

Passwords. We use them in so many areas of our lives and we all hate them. Passwords for our banking sites, for social media, our phones, and our computers. At some point, everything is protected with a password. Passwords are everywhere and yet we are still getting hacked. In addition to the password, levels of access are granted to a user based on their user name and password. For example, one user may only have access to view a record in an EMR but another user may have higher access rights and be able to edit, or even delete, the record.

Because of this access level, passwords take on higher importance. Attackers are looking for administrator level accounts so that they can install programs, edit logs, and have total control over data. From the previous section on brute force attacks, we can see why having a strong password is so important. If your passwords are weak, then no amount of security will stop an attacker.

Why is that? Because the password itself is only a protection if it is secure. But secure passwords are hard to remember and more importantly, inconvenient. Humans don't like to be inconvenienced so we tend to choose passwords that we can quickly use. That is where the problem comes in.

What makes a strong password?

So, then what is a secure password? I will explain that in detail and how to make secure passwords. But first, a little background and some of this will be a review from the previous section.

Most sites store passwords in encrypted form. Sometimes they are unencrypted, but this considered REALLY bad security. Most sites encrypt the passwords in such a way that they can't be decrypted. This is called a hash. When you log onto a site, they encrypt the password that you entered and then compare it to that hash. If that encrypted text matches, then you are given access to the site.

When hackers break into websites, they steal the database of these email addresses and password hashes. They then begin to crack them. The ones they are successful in cracking are posted online in various forms. This was seen when LinkedIn was hacked. 167 million user accounts with passwords were stolen. The password files were available online shortly thereafter. Hackers and security researchers alike all began to crack them. 98% were recovered without much work. The remaining were considered secure and resistant to hacking.

Whenever a site is hacked, these hashes will either be offered up for sale or posted online. After that, it's just a matter of time before they are cracked.

How are passwords cracked?

Before we discuss how to make a secure password, its best to explain just how passwords are cracked.

Passwords are cracked in three general methods. These are:

- Dictionary attack

- Brute forcing
- Hash matching

Dictionary Attack – This is where an attacker tries to guess a password from a generated list of passwords. These dictionary files can be found all over the Internet. Each time a new hack is announced, hackers take all of the passwords found from those accounts and add them to these dictionaries. Some of these may have billions of passwords in them. Once a password ends up in a dictionary, it is never safe again. Hackers are constantly updating these and sharing these files.

Brute Force Attack – A brute force attack is the most time consuming. It involves guessing a password over and over until you crack it. It would look something like this –

a

aa

aaa

aaaa

aaaaa

aaaaaa

aaaaaaa

aaaaaaaa

aaaaaaaa1

aaaaaaaa2

It would keep going until it exhausts every possible combination of characters for a given password length. This is resource and time intensive. That is why dictionary attacks are preferred.

Hash Matching Attack – Using the above method of brute forcing, attackers can generate a word list and then hash them. These are called Rainbow Tables. A rainbow Table will have a list of password hashes for all possible combinations of character to a given password length. The attacker would take their list of stolen password hashes and compare them to this table. It's similar to brute force but a lot quicker.

What is a secure password?

Now that we understand how passwords are cracked, we can explain how to secure them. A secure password is one that is resistant to being cracked by the methods we discussed above. Having a secure password means understanding the elements that make up that security. There are three elements that control how secure a password is.

These are:

- Password length
- Password complexity
- Password randomness

Password length is the number of character that the password contains. This is seen when you are required to make passwords that are a certain length, such as more than 8 digits.

Password complexity is what type of characters are used in the password. These can be letters, both lower and upper case, numbers, and punctuation like !@#$%^&*(). There are 26 upper letters, 26 lower letters, 10 numbers, and around 30 usable keyboard punctuation characters. This gives us 92 possible characters to use in our passwords.

Password randomness is how unique your password is. Can the password be found in a language dictionary? Don't think that if you use a word in a different language that this will protect you. Hackers have already incorporated foreign languages in their dictionaries. Is your password based on a word? Did you just change some letters to numbers? This also isn't secure because password cracking software can take that into account. It can change all E letters to 3, L to 1, etc.

Total Geek Moment:

Here is the math behind a secure password.

Using our standard keyboard, there are 92 possible characters for each digit of a password. 26 upper letters, 26 lower letters, 10 numbers and 30 symbols or punctuation. For each digit we add, the number of passwords goes up exponentially.

2-digit password = 92 x 92 (92^2) = 8,464 possible passwords

3-digit password = 92 x 92 x 92 (92^3) = 778,688 possible passwords

5-digit password = 92 x 92 x 92 x 92 x 92 (92^5) = 6,590,815,232 possible passwords

7-digit password = 92 x 92 x 92 x 92 x 92 x 92 x 92 (92^7) = 55,784,660,123,648 possible passwords

As you can see, just adding a single digit to our password greatly increases the complexity of that password. But that is also because we are using all available letters, numbers, and characters.

(Did you intend to make the coloring different between the two boxes?)

Password cracking software can crack hundreds of thousands to millions, and sometimes, billions, of passwords per second. In the 7-digit example above, a password cracker that could crack 1 million passwords per second would take 106 years to attempt all possible passwords. This can be decreased by using more powerful hardware but a truly random password that is longer is very secure.

A truly secure password would be completely random and at least 12 characters in length. Something like this –

$8f9Fus8@ca

This password would be immune to cracking for the foreseeable password. But please, don't use that one. That is just an example password.

Use both upper and lower letters, numbers, punctuation, and then make the password 12 or more characters. Don't use words or derivatives of words.

But wait... I can't remember that!

A truly secure password is difficult to remember. That is where a password manager comes in. A password manager can generate a strong and secure password for you and then store it. It allows you to create unique passwords for all of the sites you visit. The password manager stores all of these in one location and then you only need to remember the password to access your manager. Password managers will integrate with your computers, browsers, and mobile devices so you can use them anywhere. As long as the password you use to secure your password manager is strong, then you are safe.

I will cover using a password manager to secure your passwords in Part III of this book.

The Official HIPAA Jungle Map

SplashData compiles a list of the most commonly used passwords that users are choosing for their passwords. This list was compiled using breaches that have been uploaded online so the passwords are for real user accounts. I have used the first 25 passwords from their list in this book.

According to SplashData, almost 10% of users have used at least one of the 25 worst passwords on their 2018 list.

Nearly 3% of users have used the worst password, 123456.

Here is the 2018 list of most commonly used passwords.

1. **123456** (Unchanged)
2. **password** (Unchanged)
3. **123456789** (Up 3)
4. **12345678** (Down 1)
5. **12345** (Unchanged)
6. **111111** (New)
7. **1234567** (Up 1)
8. **sunshine** (New)
9. **qwerty** (Down 5)
10. **iloveyou** (Unchanged)
11. **princess** (New)
12. **admin** (Down 1)
13. **welcome** (Down 1)
14. **666666** (New)
15. **abc123** (Unchanged)
16. **football** (Down 7)

The Official HIPAA Jungle Map

17. **123123** (Unchanged)

18. **monkey** (Down 5)

19. **654321** (New)

20. **!@#$%^&*** (New)

21. **charlie** (New)

22. **aa123456** (New)

23. **donald** (New)

24. **password1** (New)

25. **qwerty123** (New)

Is your password on this list? If it is, you can see why hacks keep happening. Most people use the same passwords as each other.

These passwords would be cracked in under 10 seconds.

Password security is something that is easy to improve by simply using good passwords. In Part III, I will go over how to make strong passwords that are nearly impossible to crack.

The Official HIPAA Jungle Map

Vulnerabilities

Software has become more complex as we add more features. Windows 10 has more than 50 million lines of code. Despite their best efforts, programmers make errors. Over time, these errors are discovered either as bugs or as vulnerabilities. Vulnerabilities are holes in software that allow attackers to take over computers. Attacker create programs called exploits that make use of these vulnerabilities.

A hole that has been found but the vendor hasn't yet released a software patch for it is called a zero-day vulnerability. These are highly sought after because the vendor hasn't fixed the problem. This allows attackers a way in that is very hard to defend against. Because no one yet knows of the vulnerability, the chances of detecting an attack are very small.

Sometimes these exploits are added to malware like ransomware. The WannCry ransomware is an example of this. An exploit called EternalBlue, which had been developed by the US National Security Agency, allowed attackers to attack Windows operating systems. This exploit was added into WannaCry and because of this, allowed the ransomware to spread quickly worldwide. It was estimated that over 200,000 computers were infected worldwide. Microsoft released an emergency patch within days to fix the vulnerability. This slowed the spread of the ransomware. However, computers that didn't install the patch, were still vulnerable.

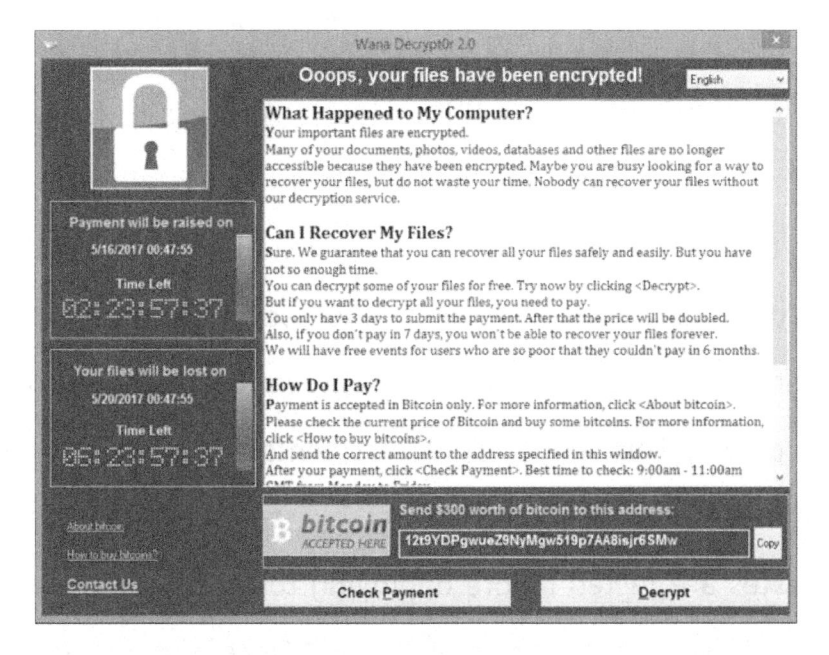

This is the window that was presented when a computer was infected with WannaCry.

Software vendors periodically release updates for their products to plug these holes. As we saw in the case of WannaCry, sometimes vendors release emergency patches due to a serious vulnerability that has been discovered. The process of keeping your computers up to date with these updates is known as patch management. For medical

The Official HIPAA Jungle Map

practices, this may include patches for your operating systems like Windows 10 or Server 2012/2016, your EMR software, and other programs like Microsoft Office.

Microsoft tried to make this an easier process to manage with Windows Update. However, this installs all updates that Microsoft thought needed to be installed. In theory, this is a good idea. However, there have been several incidents where a patch pushed out by Microsoft actually crashed computers. This is why IT departments and management companies use a controlled patch management process. Updates are tested before deploying to all computers and not allowed to be force installed. Once the update is deemed safe, it will be installed on all systems in a controlled manner to ensure that no system is missed. If one system isn't patched, a hole still exists in the network.

Installing Windows updates sometimes results in nightmares for users

In October 2018, Microsoft released an update that could use a large amount of hard drive space but could also cause your computer to crash. Many businesses returned to work to find their computers completely unusable. It would require a computer tech to help get the computer back up and running.

Unfortunately, this has happened several times to Microsoft over the years with forced updates.

https://www.forbes.com/sites/kevinmurnane/2018/09/23/installing-windows-10s-october-update-could-result-in-a-nightmare-heres-how-to-avoid-it/#7f821462512e

https://www.forbes.com/sites/gordonkelly/2016/08/15/microsoft-warns-windows-10-anniversary-update-crashes-problems/#4aefd2b77195

https://www.zdnet.com/article/microsoft-weve-fixed-windows-7-not-genuine-and-network-share-issues/

What does OCR have to say about patch management?

In its June 2018 cybersecurity newsletter, OCR outlined the HIPAA patch management requirements and why keeping software patched is an essential element of HIPAA compliance. OCR stated that patch management is "the process of identifying, acquiring, installing and verifying patches for products and systems."

"Security vulnerabilities may be present in many types of software including databases, electronic health records (EHRs), operating systems, email, applets such as Java and Adobe Flash, and device firmware. Identifying and mitigating the risks unpatched software poses to ePHI is important to ensure the protection of ePHI and in fulfilling HIPAA requirements."

OCR June 2018 cybersecurity newsletter

https://www.hhs.gov/sites/default/files/june-2018-newsletter-software-patches.pdf

Although the words patch management are not specifically mentioned in the HIPAA Security Rule, the process of identifying vulnerabilities to your practice is covered by HIPAA administrative safeguards.

Practices are required to conduct Risk Assessments to identify vulnerabilities to the confidentiality, integrity, and availability of their protected health information.

This can be found in **45 C.F.R. § 164.308(a)(1)(i)(A).**

If anything is found, it must be addressed according to practice's risk management process.

This can be found in **45 C.F.R. § 164.308(a)(1)(i)(B).**

Another area that addresses patch management is covered under the malicious software protection section of the Security Rule.

This can be found in **45 C.F.R. § 164.308(a)(5)(ii)(B).**

OCR takes this very seriously and has levied fines for practices that did not keep their software updated and led to data being compromised.

The Official HIPAA Jungle Map

Patch Management:
Not keeping your software patched is like having a backdoor into your castle. It doesn't matter how secure your network is if you don't patch your software.

Iron Comet

Copyright © 2019 Iron Comet Consulting, Inc.

Physical Breaches

Physical breaches cover a wide range of attacks. These could be as simple as a losing a single mobile device or the theft of an office's computer systems. As patient data has migrated from paper charts to electronic data, it has become easier for large amounts of data to be stolen.

This isn't one that gets the headlines very often. With all of the attention on hackers and malware, thefts and other forms of physical breaches seem to fall through the cracks. However, it is just as dangerous for a practice.

Here some examples of physical breaches:

- Misplacing a tablet or laptop that contains ePHI
- A theft where some or all computers of the practice are stolen
- Lost or stolen backup drives
- Theft of paper charts
- Lost or stolen mobile smart phone that contains ePHI
- Charts being thrown away improperly
- Employees stealing data

USB ports have made it very easy to attach many types of devices to computers. They also make it easy to attach USB flash drives that allow those with malicious intent to steal large amounts of data. Storage size on flash drives has grown larger than the databases of most practices. This makes it easy for a single flash drive to contain an entire practice's data.

The Official HIPAA Jungle Map

The same is true for mobile phones. HIPAA and mobile devices is an area that many entities fall short because it's easy to forget that these highly portable devices can contain so much information. We take for granted just how much they can carry until one goes missing.

The Catholic Health Care Services of the Archdiocese of Philadelphia (CHCS) found out the hard way when a device belonging to them was stolen. An investigation by U.S. Department of Health and Human Services Office for Civil Rights (OCR) found numerous lapses that resulted in a massive fine.

In 2014, an iPhone belong to CHCS was stolen containing the PHI of 412 patients. The device was not encrypted or password protected.

In addition, CHCS did not have any polices in place to handle HIPAA and mobile devices in their business. They had performed no Risk Assessment to know that these devices posed an enormous risk to the security if their PHI.

Furthermore, they did not have polices in place to handle a breach after a device was stolen.

The investigation by OCR resulted in a fine of $650,000 and a corrective action plan for two years.

Keep in mind that this was a breach of only 412 patients. However, since CHCS had not even performed a Risk Assessment and had no policies in place to handle this kind of breach, the fine was much higher. This sort of action could be considered willful neglect.

Healthcare has changed a great deal in the last ten years. Computers are now common place but so are mobile devices such as phones and tablets. These devices can carry an enormous amount of data on them and when lost or stolen, can cause a great deal of damage to many patients.

This is why the HIPAA Security Rule has encryption requirements. These requirements are designed to protect data on easily stolen devices such as phone, tablets, and backups. While encryption is addressable, an entity should explain why they determined it wasn't necessary to use in their situation.

When most entities think about their PHI and where it is, they usually just consider computers and servers. Mobile devices are usually forgotten. However, these devices are often a much bigger risk due to the chances of theft or being lost.

The first step is to perform a thorough Risk Assessment. Identify the threats that your practice is exposed to. What areas are the most likely? If you use mobile devices, where and when are they used? Do they leave the practice?

Once you have identified the threats, make a plan to reduce, or mitigate the risk. This is usually done by using device encryption and strong passwords. That way, if the devices are stolen or lost, the data is still safe.

Are there other areas of your practice where encryption should be used? All workstations and servers should utilize encryption, especially if your Risk Assessment identifies your area as having a higher risk to burglary or insider theft.

Before deploying mobile devices in your organization, ensure that the proper risk analysis has been performed. In addition, create the policies and procedures to protect the data on these devices. Don't let convenience cause a breach in your compliance.

According to Verizon, 25% of all healthcare organizations in the United States have had a breach due to mobile devices in 2018. As these devices become more prevalent, that number will only go up. The study also found that of the breaches involving mobile devices, 67% were found to be major breaches and of those, 40% had major repercussions where remediation was documented as being both expensive and difficult.

Based on these numbers, it appears that most organizations are not reporting these breaches as required under HIPAA regulations.

Employee Breaches

For just about every type of businesses, insiders are usually the biggest threat. This is because of their unique knowledge and access to the company. Small practices have the same issue.

Employees are often the weakest link in your practice's security plan. Because humans are well, human. We make mistakes. When your biller clicks on a phishing link, she

The Official HIPAA Jungle Map

likely didn't do it on purpose but the end result is still an infection.

However, some employee breaches are more intentional. Medical information is very private and often a tempting target. This is often very true for celebrities. The recent case of Jussie Smollett highlights this.

On January 29, 2019, Jussie Smollett alleged that he was attacked by two individuals. He was admitted into Chicago's Northwestern Memorial Hospital emergency room for injuries he sustained.

After a police investigation, it was alleged by that Mr. Smollet had staged the entire incident as a publicity stunt. He was arrested on February 21 and charged with disorderly conduct and filing a false police report.

Due to the amount of media coverage of the case, both with the initial attack and the subsequent arrest, employees of the hospital became curious and searched for Mr. Smollett's medical records. Many of them viewed the records directly.

The Official HIPAA Jungle Map

As a normal course, Northwestern Memorial Hospital reviewed its access logs for Protected Health Information (PHI). They discovered that dozens of employees had searched and accessed the records. The hospital then took action and fired every employee who viewed the records. The exact numbers are not known and the hospital hasn't commented on privacy grounds. However, several news agencies were reporting that as many as 60 have been fired.

Accessing patient information without need is a HIPAA violation.

If a medical need has not been established, then accessing the record of a patient is a HIPAA violation.

Another similar incident occurred in 2008 when 13 employees of UCLA Medical Center were fired for viewing the medical records of Britney Spears. Ms. Spears had been hospitalized in the psychiatric unit for treatment.

Celebrity records are a temptation for staff who have access to the records. The penalties can also include jail time as we saw in the case of Huping Zhou above.

As was covered in the Physical Breaches section, employees could use flash drives to steal large amounts of data. If access to charts isn't being monitored, then this would likely never be detected.

Another way an employee could breach a network is after they are fired. Access to EMRs or VPNs that have not been terminated give former employees access to patient records.

For small practices, not all breaches by an employee are malicious. Sometimes it can be something as simple as faxing patient information to the wrong number.

One Texas practice sent over patient data to a local news station by accident because the phone number of the studio was one digit different than the hospital. Luckily the news studio contacted the practice and promptly destroyed the data.

This is also an area where working with an outside billing company can be an issue. Faxing a billing company usually involves sending over large amounts of data so a breach there would be larger.

Another area to be mindful of for employees is computer monitors that are viewable by others. This is common at a front desk or checkout location. Monitors that don't use screen protectors may be visible to patients checking in or out.

Also leaving charts in areas where others, who do not have a medical need to view them, can access the chart. This can be as simple as leaving a chart at a nurse's station. The next patient could see it and this would be a breach.

Employees can cause a lot of harm to a practice even when its unintentional. While technical measures can be put in place to lower your risk, training is the best answer.

The Official HIPAA Jungle Map

Take your time and verify before you send patient records via fax...
— Iron Comet

Social Media

Social media is everywhere. It has made communicating with each other a lot easier and more convenient. However, this ease of use also makes violating HIPAA easier as well. Posting or sharing protected health information (PHI) online without approval of the patient is a HIPAA violation. HIPAA and social media don't mix very well.

The Official HIPAA Jungle Map

Gina Graziano, a patient of Northwestern Medicine Regional Medical Group (NMRMG), is currently suing for a breach of privacy of her medical records. She has alleged that a hospital employee, Jessica Wagner, accessed Graziano's medical records. Wagner then posted on Twitter about the procedures and treatments that Graziano had received at NMRMG.

The records contained sensitive information such as the reason for a recent visit to the emergency room, lab results, medications, medical history, imaging results, and other information.

"I was humiliated," Graziano said. "Embarrassed."

Jessica Wagner, as it was later discovered, is the girlfriend of Graziano's ex-boyfriend, David Worth. Wagner reviewed the records for 37 minutes on March 5 and 6 of 2018. She later provided the information to Worth.

NMRMG investigated internally and sent Graziano a letter acknowledging that inappropriate access to her records by an employee had occurred on March 5 and 6.

According to a police report, Wagner was fired for the incident.

Graziano then filed a lawsuit against NMRMG.

Attorney for Graziano, Ted Diamantopoulos said, "It's a complete invasion of my client's privacy. When a patient goes to a hospital, they expect to have their medical records private."

"They were treating me for something I didn't want anybody to know about," Graziano said. "Northwestern needs better policies in place for their staff to understand what HIPAA really means."

The following statement was released by NMRMG:

"Protecting the confidentiality of patient information is essential to our mission. Employees are trained to comply with

The Official HIPAA Jungle Map

privacy laws and face disciplinary action in accordance with our privacy policy for any violation. Regarding this specific incident, we do not comment on pending litigation."

The Department of Health and Human Services (HHS) has also been notified of the breach. This would likely trigger an investigation in this high-profile case.

This case shows two major issues when protecting patient data. The first is the issue of unauthorized access. Practices must have policies in place for employees accessing medical data. In addition, employees must be trained on these policies.

The next step is regular auditing of access logs to ensure that no one is accessing the records of those that they have no medical need to do so.

For social media, it is best to avoid all types of patient interaction. If a patient were to post that they will see the office staff on a specific day for their appointment, do not reply. This would confirm that the patient was a patient of the practice resulting in a HIPAA violation.

Social media should be used for advertising services of the practice. If a patient gives written permission to post data, such as success stories, then it would be permissible. But written patient permission would be required beforehand.

Don't let a simple mistake cost your practice in the form of lawsuits and fines.

Third Party Breaches

Often practices outsource their service needs to third parties. Under HIPAA regulations, these are known as Business Associates. But even Business Associates can outsource to others. If that second Business Associate has a breach, then it flows all the way back to the original Covered Entity.

An example of a Business Associate breach was that of North Shore - LIJ Health System, in Manhasset, N.Y. They had outsourced payment related services to a third party, Global Care delivery (GCD). GCD had 5 unencrypted laptops stolen from its Dallas office. GCD did report the breach immediately to law enforcement but did not notify their customer, North Shore until 8 months later. GCD determined that 4 of the 5 laptops did contain PHI and were not encrypted.

To make matters worse, GCD had policies in place stating that the laptops should be encrypted.

The Official HIPAA Jungle Map

This puts Covered Entities, like North Shore, in a serious situation. They are also responsible for the breach of data but they weren't informed for 8 months.

The Covered Entity is responsible for notifying HHS of the breach, as well as the local media and the patients.

Breaches by third parties can happen at any time and the practices may not be aware of them. This doesn't release the practice of the liability. Failure to report breaches can result in enormous fines.

Business Associates are not often aware of their obligations under HIPAA law and because of this, may not follow proper procedures to ensure the protection of PHI. This can also be an issue when outsourcing overseas as it makes enforcing HIPAA violations extremely difficult.

The biggest concern with Business Associates is the liability will flow back to the Covered Entity and they may never be aware of the breach. Imagine having patients contact you because they found their information online because your outsourced billing service had put it online without proper precautions. Your patients won't see it as the Business Associate's fault, they will look to blame you.

It is critical that Covered Entities properly vet their Business Associates and ensure that the Business Associate fully understands their obligations under HIPAA. A lot of this can be avoided with a pre-engagement checklist to make sure your potential Business Associates are up to the task.

Another area that is of concern to Covered Entities, as it concerns Business Associates, is cloud based EMR vendors. In January 2018, Allscripts suffered a ransomware attack. The ransomware software used was SamSam which is a favorite of attackers who focus on healthcare organizations. Nearly 1500 practices were impacted because of the attack. Many of them were down for up to six days.

One of the impacted practices, Surfside Non-Surgical Orthopedics, filed a class action lawsuit against Allscripts. The case is still pending at the time of this writing.

These types of attacks can be no fault of a practice but could still have enormous impact on a practice. Imagine not being able to access charts of patients for up to 6 days. That would make working for most practices nearly impossible.

Third party breaches are especially dangerous to practices since they may not even be aware they are happening and can't help to prevent them. However, ultimately, the Covered Entity will be responsible.

Disposing of records

Practices build up a large amount of paper data on patients. Even in the days of electronic medical records, the amount of paper that is still around can be surprising. Paper records take up a lot of space and that is often small offices are in short supply of. This often leads practices to dispose of the old records once they have been digitized. However, records containing patient data must be treated with the same care as other forms of patient data. When these paper charts are no longer needed, they must be disposed of properly, in a way that they cannot be viewed by another person. Improperly dumping patient records would result in many violations of HIPAA law. HIPAA has very specific guidelines on how these records must be destroyed when they are no longer needed. In this case study we find out what happens when a practice decided to simply throw away many of its old paper records.

In 2012, a small Denver, Colorado based pharmacy, Cornell Prescription Pharmacy, threw away the records of 1,610 patients. The records were in an unlocked dumpster on the property of the pharmacy. A local news outlet got wind of the data and contacted the Department of Health and Human services Office of Civil Rights (HHS OCR).

OCR began an investigation and found that the records had not been shredded or destroyed.

Cornell Prescription Pharmacy is a single location pharmacy. They provide in-store and prescription services to patients in the Denver metropolitan area, specializing in compounded medications and services for hospice care.

In 2015, OCR released a statement saying it had reached a settlement with the pharmacy. In their statement, OCR settled that the pharmacy had agreed to pay a $125,000 penalty and abide by a corrective action plan.

In addition to the $125,000 settlement amount, OCR required the pharmacy to develop and implement a comprehensive set of policies and procedures to comply with the Privacy Rule, and develop and provide staff training. This was done to address the deficiencies that OCR found in the pharmacy's compliance program.

"Regardless of size, organizations cannot abandon protected health information or dispose of it in dumpsters or other containers that are accessible by the public or other unauthorized persons. Even in our increasingly electronic world, it is critical that policies and procedures be in place for secure disposal of patient information, whether that information is in electronic form or on paper." OCR Director Jocelyn Samuels.

Under HIPAA regulations, patient data must be protected by a Covered Entity or Business Associate, no matter what form it takes. Paper charts are no different than electronic records.

When paper charts are thrown away in an area where anyone could access them, this information has been breached.

All records must be destroyed when no longer needed according to HIPAA regulations. If records are not disposed of properly, then the breach can result in fines ranging from $100 to $50,000 per patient record, up to a maximum of $1,500,000.

Patient records contain a lot of sensitive information that could be used for identity theft, insurance fraud, and other criminal acts.

In this case, the pharmacy wasn't a national chain. It was a single location pharmacy but it still got the attention of OCR. The government wants to make sure that all entities, regardless of their size, need to understand their obligations under HIPAA law.

Often what happens in these cases is that employees are given the responsibility of disposing of records but no budget to do so properly. The staff may not be fully trained on their obligations under HIPAA regulations and because they haven't been given a budget to handle proper disposal, will simply throw the records away. Because an employee did this, the entity is now responsible for the breach.

According to the HHS Breach Portal, there are numerous sites that have fallen prey to this violation.

Patient records from Women's Health Consultants, South Whitehall Township. The Morning Call redacted information from this photograph so no personally identifiable information is visible. (EMILY OPILO / THE MORNING CALL)

Theft or loss of devices

While we did discuss physical breaches in a section above, this section will deal more with mobile devices and backup devices that can be lost or stolen. For this section, mobile devices are defined as smartphones, tablets and laptop computers.

Because these devices are portable, we tend to carry them around with us more often. This increases the chances that they will be lost or stolen. In addition, practices are using them to store patient data. When a device that contains patient data is lost and it is not encrypted, it becomes a HIPAA violation.

HIPAA and mobile devices are an area that many entities fall short because it's easy to forget that these highly portable devices can contain so much information. We take for granted just how much they can carry until one goes missing. The Catholic Health Care Services of the Archdiocese of Philadelphia (CHCS) found out the hard way when a device belonging to them was stolen. An investigation by U.S. Department of Health and Human Services Office for Civil Rights (OCR) found numerous lapses that resulted in a massive fine.

CHCS is a healthcare business that offers management and computer services to skilled nursing homes. They performed this service as a Business Associate.

In 2014, an iPhone belong to CHCS was stolen containing the PHI of 412 patients. The device was not encrypted or password protected. This exposed the records of those patients. The data included Social Security numbers, diagnosis and treatment information, procedures, and the contact information for family members or guardians.

In addition, CHCS did not have any polices in place to handle HIPAA and mobile devices in their business. They had performed no Risk Assessment to know that these devices posed an enormous risk to the security if their PHI. Furthermore, they did not have polices in place to handle a breach after a device was stolen.

The investigation by OCR resulted in a fine of $650,000 and a corrective action plan for two years.

Keep in mind that this was a breach of only 412 patients. However, since CHCS had not even performed a Risk Assessment and had no policies in place to handle this kind of breach, the fine was much higher. This sort of action could be considered willful neglect.

"Business associates must implement the protections of the HIPAA Security Rule for the electronic protected health information they create, receive, maintain, or transmit from covered entities. This includes an enterprise-wide risk analysis and corresponding risk management plan, which are the cornerstones of the HIPAA Security Rule."

--U.S. Department of Health and Human Services Office for Civil Rights (OCR) Director Jocelyn Samuels

What do HIPAA and mobile devices have to do with each other?

Healthcare has changed a great deal in the last ten years. Computers are now common place but so are mobile devices such as phones and tablets. these devices can carry an enormous amount of data on them and when lost or stolen, can cause a great deal of damage to many patients.

This is why the HIPAA Security Rule has encryption requirements. These requirements are designed to protect data on easily stolen devices such as phone, tablets, and backups.

When most entities think about their PHI and where it is, they usually just consider computers and servers. Mobile devices are usually forgotten. However, these devices are often a much bigger risk due to the chances of theft or being lost.

According to Verizon, 25% of all healthcare organizations in the United States have had a breach due to mobile devices in 2018. As these devices become more prevalent, that number will only go up. The study also found that of the breaches involving mobile devices, 67% were found to be major breaches and of those, 40% had major repercussions where remediation was documented as being both expensive and difficult.

Based on these numbers, it appears that most organizations are not reporting these breaches as required under HIPAA regulations.

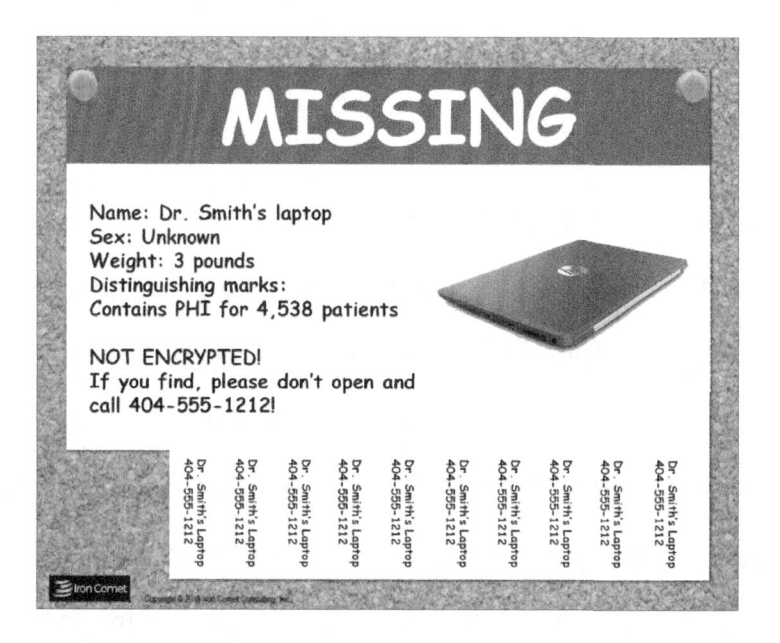

MISSING

Name: Dr. Smith's laptop
Sex: Unknown
Weight: 3 pounds
Distinguishing marks:
Contains PHI for 4,538 patients

NOT ENCRYPTED!
If you find, please don't open and call 404-555-1212!

Websites

Sometimes it easy to forget just how expansive HIPAA regulations really are. Often, we think its limited to paper records or electronic medical records. However, HIPAA covers all places that Protected Health Information exists under a Covered Entity or Business Associate's care. One place that often goes unnoticed are websites. CEs and BAs must both maintain HIPAA compliant websites.

Complete P.T., Pool & Land Physical Therapy, Inc. was posting patient testimonials about their services onto their website.

In 2012, the U.S. Department of Health and Human Services Office for Civil Rights (OCR) received a complaint that Complete P.T. had disclosed the PHI of numerous patients. They had not received prior authorization to post these testimonials and this resulted in numerous violations of HIPAA regulations. These patient testimonials including patient names and full-face photographs. They did this without first obtaining HIPAA compliant authorizations from the patients. Posting this information confirms that the patients are patients of that practice and resulted in an unauthorized disclosure of PHI.

OCR found that Compete P.T. had (quoted from OCR's press release):

Failed to reasonably safeguard PHI; Impermissibly disclosed PHI without an authorization; and Failed to implement policies and procedures with respect to PHI that were designed to comply with HIPAA's requirements with regard to authorization.

This resulted in a $25,000 fine and a corrective action plan for a period of one year. This fine was a result of not maintaining a HIPAA compliant website.

These types of violations are usually quite unintentional so it makes paying a fine for that all the more difficult. We usually associate HIPAA violations with more obvious things such as a hacked network or a stolen device. But in this case, it was something the practice never intended to do.

Many physicians use pictures and patient testimonials to market their practice. This is perfectly acceptable if HIPAA compliant authorization has been obtained from the patient before they are posted. This is standard practice for many plastic surgeons, OBGYNs and pediatricians. Before and after shots are very common.

The authorization must detail how and where the data will be used by the practice for marketing. HHS has a guideline on abiding by marketing for Covered Entities and Business Associates.

Using patient testimonials in physician marketing is a good way to attract new business. However, HHS strict guidelines on what must be done to protect patient PHI. To maintain a HIPAA compliant website, be sure that you have written authorizations from patients before posting anything. Failure to do so can result in costly fines for unintended HIPAA violations.

HIPAA is about protecting patient data. That includes their testimonials.

The reverse is also true when patients leave testimonials. Sites may wish to respond to reviews on sites like Yelp. But if you discuss anything that can be seen as an individual patient's information, it would be a HIPAA violation. Even if you are simply responding to their review. Take a look at the example review below.

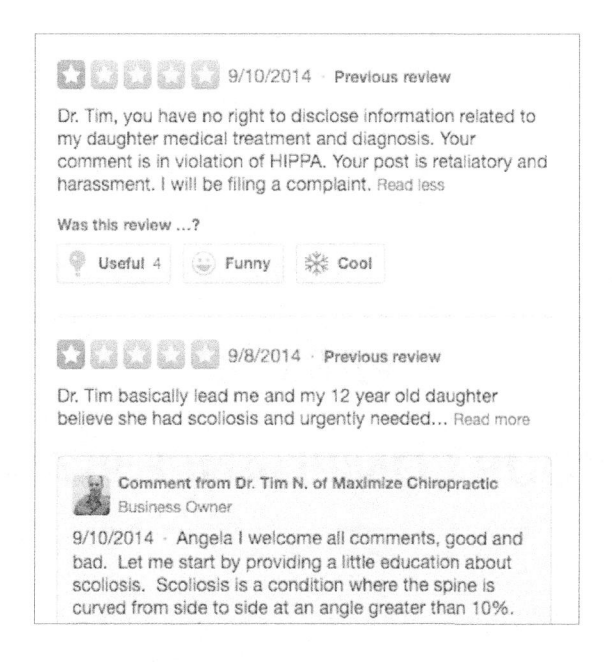

> ★☆☆☆☆ 9/10/2014 · Previous review
>
> Dr. Tim, you have no right to disclose information related to my daughter medical treatment and diagnosis. Your comment is in violation of HIPPA. Your post is retaliatory and harassment. I will be filing a complaint. Read less
>
> Was this review ...?
>
> 💡 Useful 4   😀 Funny   ❄ Cool
>
> ★☆☆☆☆ 9/8/2014 · Previous review
>
> Dr. Tim basically lead me and my 12 year old daughter believe she had scoliosis and urgently needed... Read more
>
> > Comment from Dr. Tim N. of Maximize Chiropractic
> > Business Owner
> >
> > 9/10/2014 · Angela I welcome all comments, good and bad. Let me start by providing a little education about scoliosis. Scoliosis is a condition where the spine is curved from side to side at an angle greater than 10%.

If you follow up to a review, its best just to say something like, "I am sorry you had a bad experience, please contact us so we can resolve it".

Don't confirm patient information like the physician above did.

PART III

YOUR COMPLIANCE PLAN

The Official HIPAA Jungle Map

Welcome to Part III, Your compliance plan. In this section, I will guide you through how to build a plan for your own practice. We have discussed the various threats that you face and now we will develop a plan that will address those.

Before you start, you will need to designate a Privacy Officer and a Security Officer for your practice. They can both be the same person. This will be the person in charge of handling the HIPAA process and your compliance.

Once you have done that, you can move onto the Risk Assessment.

RISK ASSESSMENT - THE STARTING POINT

Covered Entities and Business Associates must perform a yearly Risk Assessment under HIPAA law according to §164.308, the Security Rule. It was first added in 2003 in the Privacy Rule but was later expanded by the HIPAA Security Rule to cover the Administrative, physical, and technical safeguards. This was further updated by the Final Omnibus Rule to include Business Associates in the mandate to conduct a Risk Assessment. The expansion in HITECH also increased the fines that both Covered Entities and Business Associates could be assessed for non-compliance with HIPAA.

What is a Risk Assessment?

A Risk Assessment, under HIPAA regulations, is meant to be the starting point for your compliance. A Risk Assessment will show you the areas where your organization's Protected Health Information (PHI) may be at risk, what your likely threats are, your current protective measures, and where you need to improve. The purpose of a Risk Assessment is to create a road map for your HIPAA compliance. It is the starting point; you can't be compliant without a Risk Assessment.

One of the points of confusion for those that must perform a Risk Assessment is that there are no specific guidelines issued by the US Department of Health and Human Services for one. The main reason for this is that all Covered Entities and Business Associates differ greatly in size and complexity. Imagine trying to use a Risk Assessment template for a hospital for a small practice. It doesn't fit.

What HHS does provide is the ultimate goal of what should be achieved by a Risk Assessment. A Risk Assessment should identify potential risks and vulnerabilities to the confidentiality, integrity, and availability of the PHI that an organization creates, receives, maintains or transmits.

One of the most common frameworks in cybersecurity for Risk Assessment is the one created by the National Institute of Standards and Technology (NIST). It is a comprehensive approach to security and can be tailored to most organizations. The NIST Cybersecurity Framework is broken into the following parts:

- **Identify** - "Develop the organizational understanding to manage cybersecurity risk to systems, assets, data, and capabilities."

- **Protect** - "Develop and implement the appropriate safeguards to ensure delivery of critical infrastructure services."

- **Detect** - "Develop and implement the appropriate activities to identify the occurrence of a cybersecurity event."

- **Respond** - "Develop and implement the appropriate activities to take action regarding a detected cybersecurity event."

- **Recover** - "Develop and implement the appropriate activities to maintain plans for resilience and to restore any capabilities or services that were impaired due to a cybersecurity event."

The Official HIPAA Jungle Map

The Risk Assessment is the Identify part of the framework. At this stage, an organization will identify where the ePHI resides within their organization. Depending on your own situation, this could be a lot of places or in a few. But rest assured, you have ePHI in your organization.

Once you identify the places that ePHI resides, you must assess the risks that this ePHI is under. Is your entity in a high crime area? If so, then theft of your hardware is a possibility. How likely is your data to be accessed incorrectly by employees? Are hackers a threat to you? In this modern age, hackers are a threat to every practice. Nearly 50% of all breaches reported happened due to a hacking incident.

Are natural disasters a possibility? This impacts the availability portion of the data. If a tornado destroys your practice, how can you recover the data and make it available again? Risk isn't always about hackers or rogue insiders.

The main purpose here is to decide, given your own specific circumstances, what are your "reasonably anticipated" threats? Offices in Miami aren't worried about earthquakes and those in Minnesota aren't worried about hurricanes.

When you have these threats, give them a score on the likelihood of being compromised and what a compromise would mean for your organization. Would it be a total breach of all patient data or single records?

After you have assessed your threats, you need to look at the current measures you have in place to mitigate the threats. Where are they lacking? What needs to be improved?

Document everything in your final Risk Assessment. It should include the following:

- Where is your ePHI?
- What are the threats?
- Score the threats on the likelihood
- What are your current protective measures?
- What needs to be changed or fixed?

The cloud doesn't remove ePHI responsibility.

Because of confusion about how ePHI works, some providers think that if they are using a cloud-based EMR, they don't have ePHI on their systems. Because of this, they may think HIPAA no longer applies to them. Unfortunately, this is completely incorrect. Even if a practice uses a cloud-based EMR, they will have ePHI on their local systems. Faxes are still received locally whether via paper or electronically. Patients will bring in information that must be scanned in. Some sites may be using paper forms for patient intake that will be scanned into the EMR. Also, some insurance payers will send paper remits to the office. All of these once scanned in, are stored locally on computers.

In addition, if an attacker were to breach the practice's network, for example, with a phishing attack, and capture the login credentials for the practice's cloud-based EMR, who would be responsible for the breach? The breach didn't occur at the EMR. It occurred at the practice because of the lack of protection and possibly, training. The practice would be the responsible entity.

Insurance won't save you

Another common belief is that having cybersecurity insurance will protect you if a breach happens. This isn't the case if you haven't performed your Risk Assessment and your due diligence. When applying for cybersecurity insurance, insurance companies require that you perform a Risk Assessment and document it. You must provide this to them before coverage will be issued. An example where a Covered Entity stated that they had a Risk Assessment but didn't can be seen with Cottage Healthcare. They indicated that a Risk Assessment had been performed to their insurance company. After a breach, the insurance company investigated and found that an assessment had not been performed and denied to pay the claim. Insurance companies want you to be secure. So, they require you to follow the law. They aren't there so that Covered Entities (or Business Associates) can transfer all risk to them.

The Risk Assessment is just the starting point

After you have completed your Risk Assessment, you need to remediate any of the deficiencies it found. This is a critical point that many organizations often overlook. The Risk Assessment alone isn't enough. **If it finds deficiencies, they must be addressed.** Otherwise, you really didn't do anything to protect your ePHI. Knowing you have deficiencies but not addressing them is worse than not knowing. This could possibly be seen as Willful Neglect.

After you have remediated all of the issues discovered in your Risk Assessment, perform another Risk Assessment so you can document that you found the issues and corrected them. Be sure to keep both copies in your HIPAA documentation. This will show that you did fulfilled your responsibility by performing an initial assessment, resolving the issues it found, and then followed up with a final assessment to show the issues were resolved.

Each year after you perform a new Risk Assessment. Be sure to keep all of the previous ones together. HHS will ask for all Risk Assessment in a given period in the event you are audited.

> **MAJOR CAVEAT:**
>
> A Risk Assessment isn't only needed yearly. If something changes on your network, then a new assessment must be done. What are changes on a network?
>
> A new firewall
>
> A new server
>
> New computers
>
> New EMR
>
> New IT service company
>
> Adding remote access capability so employees can work from outside the practice
>
> Adding an interface to your EMR such as a hospital or lab
>
> Shifting from inside to a third-party biller
>
> This isn't an exhaustive list but it should give you an idea of what would require you to perform a new Risk Assessment.

> Keep all assessments together if your HIPAA documentation.

What are the fines for not performing a Risk Assessment?

A specific case that can be cited is that of North Memorial Health Care of Minnesota. They were fined $1.55 million for failing to perform a Risk Assessment.

Your HIPAA compliance To Do:

Perform you're your initial Risk Assessment. Make sure you are honest with yourself about what possible dangers exist. This is the hard part as it's easy to think that something doesn't apply or wouldn't happen. This will give you a false sense of security. This is the reason most practices hire outside companies to perform their Risk Assessments. This will give a non-biased assessment as to where things really stand with your practice.

Document all of the areas that need to be addressed.

Begin resolving all of the items that you identified in your initial Risk Assessment. If something cannot be addressed, notate that in your documentation.

After you have resolved all of the items found, perform a second Risk Assessment to ensure that everything has been addressed. Keep copies of both Risk Assessments in your HIPAA documentation.

NETWORK AND COMPUTER SECURITY

Firewalls

A firewall is hardware device (and in some cases, a software program) that separates one network from the Internet. It then watches all traffic coming and going for signs of attacks. It can also watch for large amounts of data leaving a network, such as in the case of a breach. If an attacker is trying to steal patient records, a monitored firewall will see that.

Modern firewalls are known as Unified Threat Management devices. This means that they are more than just firewalls. They will also include Intrusion Detection Systems (IDS) and Intrusion Prevention Systems (IPS). There can also be other services provided such as spam filtering, Virtual Private Network (VPN) access, and traffic filtering.

Firewalls are the first step to keeping attackers out of a network.

How do firewalls work?

Any device that uses networking, uses a system called TCP/IP. This is the networking protocol of the internet. TCP/IP works by assigning an IP address to all devices and then using ports to make connections to those IP addresses. A port is where a service runs to handle a connection. For example, if you wanted to visit a web page, you would be using port 80. If the web page is using encryption, like your banking site, it will use port 443.

You can think of ports as doors in your house. They are there to allow specific traffic into and out of your network.

An attacker will use a program known as a port scanner to scan the outside of your network for any of these ports. If they find an open port, they will see what service is running on that port. It could be email, a web server, local networking for your workstations, a printer, your EMR server, or many other services. Once they have discovered what service is running, the attacker will attempt to exploit any weaknesses in that service. This may be with brute force password guessing or seeing if the service is vulnerable to exploits.

A firewall works by blocking unnecessary ports and filtering traffic on the ones that must be open. It will inspect the traffic to see if it is allowed based on a series of rules the firewall has.

The most important place for a firewall is at your network's edge, right behind your internet connection. This way, it can filter all traffic that is coming into your practice. Think of the firewall as a security guard for your network.

Software firewalls can also protect servers and workstations from attacks on a local network. Microsoft Windows includes a software firewall with their operating systems. These firewalls help to stop attacks against specific devices on your network.

When is a firewall NOT a firewall?

A lot of confusion can be found with firewalls and routers. The reason is that there is no set standard on just what qualifies as a firewall. Many consumer grade routers market themselves firewalls. But the reality is that simply blocking traffic to a device doesn't make it a firewall. A true firewall is hardened to attacks and performs a great many services to protect a network. Consumer grade routers just don't do that.

Consumer grade routers are the ones you can buy at Best Buy, Walmart, etc. to provide wireless networking to your home or office. They are easy to install and get up and running. Because of this, they have been installed across many small businesses and practices.

A D-Link consumer grade wireless router

The Official HIPAA Jungle Map

The biggest reason this is such a huge problem is that manufacturers of these devices aren't concerned about security.

Does your office use a consumer router from one of the following vendors as its access to the Internet?

- D-Link
- TP-Link
- Netgear
- Linksys
- Asus
- AVM
- Belkin
- Cerio
- TrendNet
- Zyxel

A new report from The American Consumer Institute will make you wish you weren't using one. A sampling of 186 routers were taken from the manufacturers above and they found an astonishing 83% were vulnerable to remote attack. These would be attacks from outside your network, or across the Internet. A total of 32,003 vulnerabilities were found with an average of **172 PER router**.

The Official HIPAA Jungle Map

What this means is that just about any consumer router you can buy online, at Best Buy, Walmart, or similar locations is vulnerable.

These routers have vulnerabilities that allow a remote attacker to compromise the device. This would allow remote attackers to gain access to your practice's network. These devices weren't designed with in depth logging or ways to alert users of an attack. An attacker would be able to bypass the router and steal ePHI without a practice ever knowing.

The main reason for these issues is that consumer routers were never intended to protect a business or practice. They were originally designed to provide internet access to a home. No effort was made to add security to these devices and, over time, the threats have become more plentiful and dangerous.

Again, these devices are not firewalls and won't protect you from the bad things on the Internet. For that, a business level firewall is required.

Another issue is that when these routers have updates, most practices don't install them. Even though a vulnerability may have been patched, most offices still run on the older, unpatched software. Patching your router is not something most people think about.

Why is not having a firewall a HIPAA violation?

Since HIPAA requires that a Covered Entity or Business Associate take? all reasonable and appropriate steps to protect Protected Health Information (PHI), this means that sites must use firewall technology. The confusion often comes in when practices purchase consumer grade routers that claim firewall technology built it. These devices offer little protection and will not keep out attackers. They certainly weren't designed to protect networks that contain ePHI.

In addition, the firewalls must be monitored. Not monitoring a firewall is like having an alarm system that doesn't call the police when it goes off. Its virtually useless. Watching the log files for signs of an attack can help prevent attacks from being successful.

Since firewalls are an integral part of network security, you can't achieve HIPAA compliance without one. Not having one becomes a HIPAA violation by itself.

Your HIPAA compliance To Do:

Make sure your practice has a real firewall in place. Example brands would be:

- SonicWall
- pfSense
- Cisco

Each of these brands also add in intrusion detection and prevention, along with other protective services.

One item to note, brands such as SonicWall and Cisco will require an annual subscription for some of their services to operate. I prefer pfSense firewalls for the sites I manage because it doesn't require this.

Ensure that the firewall is installed and working properly.

Keep your firewall up to date with patches from the vendor.

Regularly view the logs of your device to make sure that attacks aren't getting through. This can be a tedious process and it is probably better left to your IT person. Firewall logs can be difficult to understand but must be checked. Like I said before, having a firewall that no one watches is like having an alarm system that isn't being monitored.

Backups and Disaster Recovery

One of the most important parts of cybersecurity is actually having a backup and disaster recovery plan in place. This is often the area that many practices overlook because it may involve someone needing to be involved and this makes it easier to be forgotten. But what's worse than thinking you have a good disaster plan in place? Having one that doesn't actually protect your business at all. This is what happened to Apex HCM in early 2019. Ransomware managed to make its way onto their network and their backup and disaster recovery system wasn't able to help them

Roswell, Georgia based Apex HCH was infected with ransomware. Apex HCH is a cloud-based payroll company that provides services to payroll service companies, who in turn, provide services to small and mid-sized businesses. The ransomware encrypted all of the data on their main systems incredibly fast. It then demanded payment to provide the company with a key to unlock their data.

At this point, most companies would resort to their backup and disaster recovery plan to help restore the data and operations. The company pulled all the infected servers offline and started the process of notifying its customers of the breach. According to Brian Krebs, a security author, the ransomware never touched the customers of Apex HCH's data. Instead, it infected all of the internal systems of the company and this made it impossible to run operations. Krebs reached out to Apex and spoke with Ian Oxman who is the company's chief marketing officer. Oxman had this to say:

"We had just recently completed a pretty state-of-the-art disaster recovery plan off-site and out of state that was mirroring our live system," Oxman said. *"But when the ransomware bomb went off, not only did it go through and infect our own network, it was then immediately picked up in our disaster recovery site, which made switching over to that site unusable."*

Let that sink in for a moment.

The company thought they had just implemented a thorough, state of the art, backup and disaster recovery plan. They thought that they had this all covered. But due to poor implementation, the system didn't work. After several days of trying to restore the data, at the advisement of computer security firms, Apex HCH paid the ransom.

However, even paying the ransom didn't solve the problem. The ransomware didn't restore the data in its original state.

Some of the programs that were infected were rendered unusable even after decryption. This, in turn, delayed the restoration process.

The company did not disclose how much was paid as ransom.

It should be of concern to business owners that even paying a ransom may not get them back up and running. Many companies don't have a backup or disaster recovery plan in place. When they do get infected with ransomware, the only option is to pay. However, if that won't deliver the promised result of restoring the business, then the business is out of options. That is why having a good backup disaster recovery plan is so crucial for any business, but especially so for small businesses who often lack the resources of larger businesses.

What is a backup and disaster recovery plan?

A backup and disaster recovery (also called BDR) plan is the documented process a company will follow should they need to restore their data operations in the event that data becomes unusable. Most people think of this as happening when a hacker attacks a company, however, another need for BDR is in natural disasters or robbery. If you arrived at your office to find that all the computers had been stolen, would you be able to restore and be back up and running? How long would it take?

Our data has now become too important to how our businesses run to be handled without proper backups in place.

3..2..1.. ready for reliable backup disaster recovery plan?

The most reliable way to protect your practice's data is to use the 3 2 1 system for backups. This means:

- 3 separate backups of the data
- 2 different types of backups (two different mediums)
- 1 backup offsite

3-2-1 Rule for Backup and Disaster Recovery

3 — Three copies of your data, your original data and two copies of it

2 — Store two copies on two different media

1 — One copy of your data is stored offsite

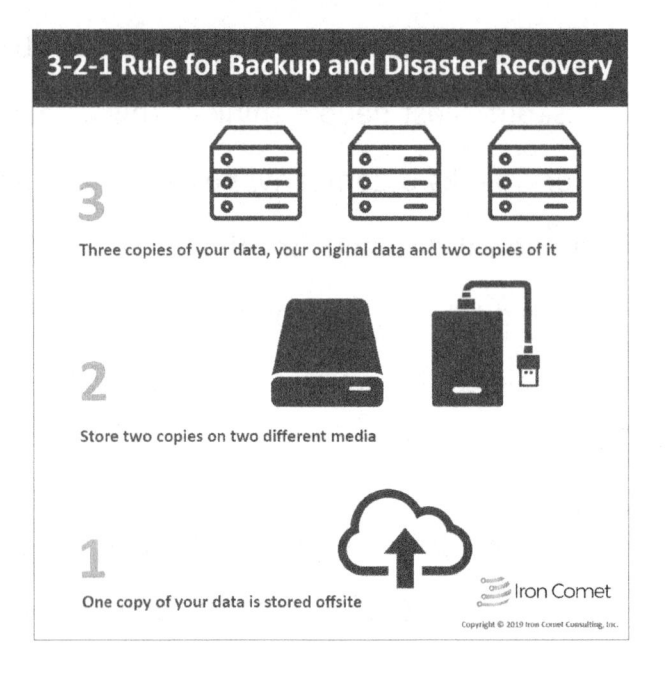

Iron Comet
Copyright © 2019 Iron Comet Consulting, Inc.

This system protects your data from many different forms of attacks but also in the event of a natural disaster or robbery.

Your main data is stored on the server in your office. That is your original data. From there, you would have an external hard drive that is plugged into the server. It backs up at a specific time each day, not in real time. At the end of the day, these drives are swapped and one is taken offsite.

3 – We have the original data and 2 additional copies

2 – The data is on the server and external hard drives (2 different media)

1 – One of the drives is always offsite

Using a cloud service would be an alternative to swapping external drives daily. The amount of data would be the determining factor of if this was a realistic option for your practice. If you have a very large amount of data that is only available in the cloud, it could take a very long time to download and retrieve your data in when needed. This could take several days. This is especially true of the cheaper cloud service offerings. With more expansive options, the data storage company will send you a hard drive that contains your data so that you can be back up and running quickly. However, this increase in service does come with an increase in cost. A lot of practices try to save money by using lower end cloud backup companies that are more designed for the home user and not a busy practice.

Another determining factor when choosing a cloud backup provider is whether they will sign a Business Associate

The Official HIPAA Jungle Map

Agreement for you. If they won't, then you won't be able to use them.

For most small practices, you won't need real-time backup. This is important for those that don't have a dedicated IT person on staff to make sure that ransomware doesn't make it to the backups. Ideally, you would want to have one backup that is not connected anywhere at any time. For example, the external drive that is offsite and not connected to any computer. If you were infected with ransomware, that backup would not be impacted. A cloud backup could become infected if the ransomware isn't noticed and the infected data is copied to the cloud, overwriting your good data.

Protecting our data is becoming harder based on the nature of the threats we all face. Ransomware attacks have increased dramatically since they were first discovered. By implementing a multi-level approach to protecting your data, like the 3-2-1 system, you will prevent these issues from happening.

The Official HIPAA Jungle Map

Your HIPAA compliance To Do:

Determine what data needs to be backed up in your practice. Even if you are using a cloud based EMR, you will have data on your network that needs to be protected. Build your list and be sure you go through every part of your network to ensure that nothing important is missed.

Who will be responsible for making sure the backups run and are performing as needed?

Decide on how you will backup the data you have. What devices will you use? External hard drives, network attached storage (NAS) device, cloud storage?

Create a backup map that shows what data is being backed up and where it is going. This will be filed in your HIPAA documentation. See example below.

Put your system together using the methods you have chosen. Decide on when backups will run, at night, etc.

Configure your backup software to run.

The Official HIPAA Jungle Map

Run a test of your backup system. Did it work as you planned? If not, make any necessary adjustments.

Run a full backup of all of your data.

Check your backup status often to ensure that it is performing without errors. If errors are found, address them.

Finally, periodically, one or twice per year, use your backups to perform a full restore of your systems. This will ensure that your backup system is really working as you designed.

Following these steps will ensure you have a robust system in place to protect your practice.

An example data backup map is on the next page.

The Official HIPAA Jungle Map

Data Backup Map and Plan

Customer Name:	
Responsible for backup:	Practice ☐ Iron Comet ☐ Other ☐
Backup Method:	USB Drives ☐ NAS ☐ Cloud/Online ☐ Computer on network ☐
Data Retention Period:	

Assets	Location

What is being backed up?	Where is it going?	Frequency

The Official HIPAA Jungle Map

Our backup plan involves a lot of running around, panic, and screaming...
— Iron Comet

Passwords

In the past, most people only needed to remember a couple of passwords and PIN numbers in their daily lives. However, as we use more and more online services such as banks and social media, the number of passwords we need has increased dramatically. This has created a situation where the average user simply uses the same password, or a slight derivative of it, for all of their online accounts. This creates a security situation since once one account is breached, that same password can be used to access other services the user might have. This problem is what password managers were designed to solve. The best password manager for most users and the medical office staff is LastPass. It is easy to set up and uses and the free version provides all the basic features that nearly everyone would need.

We have too many passwords to remember. And humans aren't good at remembering random things. This means we tend to choose passwords that are meaningful to us and then we use them over and over again. Imagine you use a password for a site like Marriott. Marriott was recently hacked by unknown attackers. Now your password is in the hands of the attackers. If you follow what most people do, you didn't choose a very strong password. This where a password manager can help.

So, what exactly is a password manager and why do we need one? As mentioned above, the average user today has a lot more passwords to remember that before. This creates a situation where most people use the same password over and over. A password manager solves this by creating a unique password for each site you use. It then stores that password in an encrypted database that only you can use. Each time you access the site, the password manager will insert the password in for you. You no longer have to remember the password at all. In addition, the password manager generates completely random and extremely secure passwords so they are very resistant to hacking. Now you only need to remember one password – the password to the database of your password manager.

Most password managers integrate directly into your browsers and also have mobile apps. This means that you can use your secure passwords now anywhere you go.

LastPass is a free password manager. It integrates with all major browsers such as Microsoft Edge, Google Chrome, Mozilla Firefox, and Apple Safari. It also has mobile apps for both Android and Apple IOS. This means it is used anywhere you will need it. If it's available, you are more likely to use it.

The Official HIPAA Jungle Map

LastPass has a free version and a premium version that has more features. However, for most users, the free version is enough.

Below is the menu for LastPass in a Chrome browser.

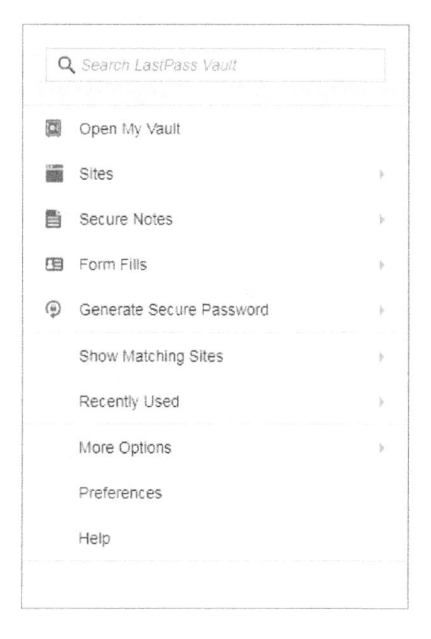

```
Search LastPass Vault
Open My Vault
Sites
Secure Notes
Form Fills
Generate Secure Password
Show Matching Sites
Recently Used
More Options
Preferences
Help
```

This menu gives you access to all of the functions within LastPass. From here you can generate completely secure and random passwords. They are all stored in your LastPass vault. As long as you have chosen a strong master password for this vault, your passwords will remain secure.

The Official HIPAA Jungle Map

You can also store passwords for things like your WIFI routers and other types of passwords under the Secure Notes section. This would be used for passwords that are not automatically entered into a site for you.

Another feature of LastPass that is useful is the Form Fill. This allows you to save the registration information you have to enter into a new site. Your name, address, and email address can be stored securely and then when you wanted it entered, you can do so quickly.

LastPass is available just about anywhere you would need it: your computer browsers, mobile devices, and tablets. The more places you can use it, the more likely you will. It integrates itself in such a way that it makes it very easy to generate passwords when you need them. Also, it can be set to automatically insert them when you visit the site.

It is highly recommended that practices use strong passwords for all of their sites such as payment portals and even electronic medical records (EMRs). However, LastPass has a final feature that is very helpful to practices. It allows for shared passwords. This means that a practice manager could generate passwords for sites and then share them with the LastPass of other employees of the practice. But this sharing doesn't actually give the employee access to the password. This is very useful when an employee leaves as you wouldn't need to change the password. You would just revoke their shared access to it.

This feature allows you to keep control of your practice's passwords and not fear that an employee could use it outside of the office.

You can download LastPass at:

https://www.lastpass.com

Your HIPAA compliance To Do:

Download the LastPass browser extension for your browser (Chrome, Firefox, Safari, etc.)

Create a strong master password for Lastpass

Setup each of your online sites with a new, secure password that is randomly generated, at least 12 characters in length

If you need to share access to come sites, make sure your staff also has LastPass installed on their computers as well. And then share the account with them inside of LastPass. This will allow them to use the site without knowing the password.

Server and workstation security

A server is a computer on your network that acts as a central location for user authentication, network management, and stores data. What does that mean for your small practice?

One of the common items I hear when dealing with small practices is that they went to the cloud for their EMR because they didn't want to have a server. While it's true, you wouldn't need a robust server if you are using a cloud based EMR, you still need a server.

The Official HIPAA Jungle Map

Why is that?

Some of the requirements of the HIPAA Security Rule are access controls, unique user identification, and audit controls. Even if you are using a cloud based EMR, users on your network must be uniquely identified so that all of their activity is logged. In addition, not all users need the same level of access to information. A server controls this by proving each user with its access rights.

Password polices must be in place for the practice. This means setting a standard on what type and length of passwords can be used by users. These are all set on a policy in a server. In windows networks, these are known as domain policies. Additional settings would be how long a PC will sit idle before it locks the screen, the type of screensaver that can be shown, and a logon warning.

To do all of these items, you must have a domain controller server. While HIPAA regulations do not specifically say a server must be used, there is no other way to achieve these goals without one. There are ways to host the server as a virtual server in the cloud but over time, this option won't be cost effective for a small practice.

A domain controller would be a small server that runs a Windows Server operating system. Current acceptable versions are Windows Server 2012, Windows Server 2016, and Windows Server 2019. The hardware requirements for a domain controller only wouldn't be expensive for a small practice. In many cases, it can handle multiple roles such as a fax server, file storage, remote access server, and log management server.

What policies do you need to setup for your practice?

Password policies –

- Password length and complexity – how strong and secure are your passwords?
- Password expiration – how often do password need to be changed?
- Password reuse – can a user use the same password as they have used before?

The Official HIPAA Jungle Map

Logging and user management –

- User log on and log off – who is logging on/off and when
- User access to resources – what are users accessing on your network? Printers, files, programs
- New users created or changed
- User passwords changed
- Users elevating privileges – are users being added to the administrator's group?
- Users being deleted
- User management – when employees leave, their access needs to be removed
- Users installing programs
- New programs installed on server
- User rights – what can a user access and what can they not
- Backup failures
- Remote access – who is allowed to connect remotely?

Domain wide policies –

- Idle computer log off time
- Screensavers
- Network logon warnings – advising that this computer is for official work only and not personal use or non-employee use

All of these items can be managed from a central domain controller. If you were on the business end of a HIPAA audit, you would want to be able to provide all of this information easily. In addition, your Risk Assessment should show your policies on each of these items.

For example, our passwords are resistant to cracking because we require all passwords to be a mix of upper and lower letters, numbers, and special characters. They must be 10 or more digits long. Passwords will be changed every 90 days and users aren't able to re-use their 5 past passwords.

Your server is now collecting a lot of data on users and how they access your computers. Is anyone watching it? This is also a necessary component of security management. Logs don't mean anything if someone isn't watching to respond. If an attacker has managed to breach your network, there will be lots of signs in your log files. This is the place to watch for breaches.

Server Protection

The most important part of your server protection is to use strong passwords for your administrator users. These users have the ability to do anything on the server and network so ensuring strong password security for these accounts is critical.

Servers should be in a secure location in the practice. This doesn't mean in a corner of a backroom. They should be in an area that can be locked and secured at all times.

If you are not using USB external drives for your backup, consider disabling USB ports so that someone can't simply plug a USB device into the computer.

A free utility called USB Disks Access Manager can make this easy for you.

This would allow you to turn on and off the ability to use USB storage devices. You also don't need to reboot.

This does not stop USB from being used for other devices like printers and keyboards. It just stops drives from being usable if they are plugged into the server.

You can download it from here:

http://www.wenovo.com/freeware/usb-disks-access-manager-freeware.php

Consider using the disk encryption built into Windows server. BitLocker can encrypt the entire hard drive and its free. This will protect your server's data in the event the server itself is stolen.

Install endpoint protection software on your server. This will be anti-malware software (anti-virus software) and also intrusion detection/prevention.

Good examples include:

- Webroot
- Symantec Endpoint Protection
- Bitdefender

This will protect your server from malware attacks, as well as, many hacker attacks. Hackers usually upload tools to the machines they are compromising. Good end point protection software will catch these and quarantine them. In addition, it will look for suspicious activity and attempt to block it. Keep in mind that it also generates logs and should be monitored for attacks.

The Official HIPAA Jungle Map

Keep servers up to date with patches from Microsoft. I will cover this more in depth in a later section. However, it is very important to ensure that all patches that have been provided by Microsoft are installed. This will plug holes in your server's overall security.

Some quick tips:

Rename the domain administrator account. Don't leave it as administrator.

Remove remote administration from your server. If this is for a small practice, it shouldn't be difficult to perform all admin functions from the server itself. If you have multiple locations, this should be skipped.

Any time someone needs access to the server, it should be documented in your HIPAA documentation. Who they are, what time they needed access and for what purpose.

Workstation Security

Just like for your servers, the most important part of your workstation protection is to use strong passwords. This isn't

The Official HIPAA Jungle Map

just for the local administrator accounts, but also for users. Local administrator accounts are not as powerful as the domain administrators but do have full control over the local machine.

Disable USB ports for disk access unless you absolutely need it on workstations. This will prevent employees from plugging in USB flash drives into the computers. This will protect against malware and also data theft.

A free utility called USB Disks Access Manager can make this easy for you.

This would allow you to turn on and off the ability to use USB storage devices. You also don't need to reboot.

This doesn't not stop USB from being used for other devices like printers and keyboards. It just stops drives from being usable if they are plugged into the workstations.

You can download it from here:

http://www.wenovo.com/freeware/usb-disks-access-manager-freeware.php

Consider using the disk encryption built into Windows. BitLocker can encrypt the entire hard drive and its free. This will protect your workstation's data in the event the computer itself is stolen.

Install endpoint protection software on your server. This will be anti-malware software (anti-virus software) and also intrusion detection/prevention.

Good examples include:

- Webroot
- Symantec Endpoint Protection
- Bitdefender

This will protect your workstations from malware attacks, as well as, many hacker attacks. Hackers usually upload tools to the machines they are compromising. Good end point protection software will catch these and quarantine them. In addition, it will look for suspicious activity and attempt to block it. Keep in mind that it also generates logs and should be monitored for attacks.

Keep workstations up to date with patches from Microsoft. I will cover this more in depth in a later section. However, it is very important to ensure that all patches that have been provided by Microsoft are installed. This will plug holes in your workstation's overall security.

The Official HIPAA Jungle Map

Your HIPAA compliance To Do:

Install anti-malware software on all workstations and servers

Use strong passwords for all accounts but especially administrator accounts

Use disk encryption on servers and workstations

Set polices on your domain for passwords, auditing, and workstation security

Consider disabling USB ports for hard drive access on computers where it isn't needed

Software Updates

For most small practices, the HIPAA compliance requirements can seem very confusing. Sometimes they may not even make sense. One of these is the requirement that all software used by both Covered Entities or Business Associates be supported by the manufacturer and also kept up to date. If the software is working, why do we need to update it? Why can't an entity still use Windows XP when it's working just fine?

Anchorage Community Mental Health Services (ACMHS), a five-facility mental health organization, suffered a malware attack in 2012. They reported it to HHS in March of that year stating that the breach had affected 2,743 patients.

HHS investigated the breach and found that they failed to follow HIPAA compliance requirements to protect PHI and this led to the breach.

"Successful HIPAA compliance requires a common sense approach to assessing and addressing the risks to ePHI on a

regular basis. This includes reviewing systems for unpatched vulnerabilities and unsupported software that can leave patient information susceptible to malware and other risks."

--OCR Director Jocelyn Samuels

This means that OCR found that ACMHS had not followed through on their obligations to protect patient data because they were using software that was no longer supported and they didn't patch their software with updates. This led to the malware attack that, in turn, resulted in the breach.

ACMHS was fined $150,000 for the breach. In addition, they were required to implement a practice-wide corrective action plan. In addition, they were required to keep OCR updated on their compliance program.

$150,000 fine for not updating your software. It would have been far cheaper to pay the software vendor for the newest software than to pay the fine.

Why does unsupported software violate HIPAA compliance requirements?

Software is becoming more and more complex with each new release. As we add new functions and services into software, it increases the complexity. This includes all software from our operating systems, like Microsoft Windows, to electronic medical records. The complexity also increases the number of bugs and potential vulnerabilities in the software. Windows 7, one of Microsoft's most popular operating systems ever had over 1000 bugs patched since its initial release.

Over time, vendors release patches to address individual bugs or new versions to address a lot of them. These patches, once installed, plug the hole and ensure that the vulnerability cannot be used by an attacker. However, when entities don't apply these patches, it allows malware to attack and infect networks, even when those networks have anti-malware software.

Also, when a vendor stops supporting software due to its age, they won't be releasing any new security updates for it. For this reason, HIPAA compliance requirements state that entities must use supported software to remain in compliance.

A good example of this is the approaching end of support for Windows 7. On January 14, 2020, all support for Windows 7 will stop. Any Windows 7 machines on your network at that time will be a HIPAA violation.

Zero Day vulnerabilities a real challenge for practices and vendors

The worst offenders are called Zero-day vulnerabilities. These are newly found vulnerabilities in software that attackers quickly create their methods of exploiting. Because vendors haven't had time to release the patch, there is a space of time that allows attackers to take advantage and compromise systems. When those systems contain PHI, the results are devastating.

The WannaCry ransomware that was released in 2017 is a good example of this in action.

HHS OCR released a newsletter in June of 2018 that addressed this issue concerning software holes. You can find that report here:

https://www.hhs.gov/sites/default/files/june-2018-newsletter-software-patches.pdf

What can you do for your practice?

Patch management is a tedious process. Some patches work as expected while others cause new issues on the computers they are installed on. Even Microsoft has these issues.

However, this can't be a reason not to install necessary patches for your practice. It is imperative that patches be installed to patch security vulnerabilities.

In addition, install any new updates from your EMR vendors or other software that your practice uses.

When a program that your practice uses is no longer supported, you will need to either upgrade to the newest version or stop using it. Otherwise, you will have a HIPAA violation. As in the case of ACMHS, it can be an expensive violation as well.

Your HIPAA compliance To Do:

Establish where your computers currently are with patch updates. What version of Windows are you using? If you are using any version of Windows older than Windows 8, its time to upgrade.

From there, install all critical updates to your computers. If you haven't done this, this may take a while as there will be a lot of updates to download and install.

You will also need to do the same for your server. Be sure to do this after hours as all computers, including your server, may need to be rebooted more than once during this process.

The Official HIPAA Jungle Map

Follow up once per month to ensure that all updates are being installed.

Sometimes updates do come out from Microsoft that can cause issues. It's usually best to allow a third party to handle this for you as they will have tools that can filter out updates that have been known to cause issues.

In addition to your operating systems, you will need to make sure that your EMR or practice management software is the most current available from the vendor. If you are using a version that is no longer supported, it is a HIPAA violation.

For cloud based EMRs, this isn't an issue as you will always have the most current version. This applies to those using server based EMRs or practice management software.

Ensuring that your software is kept up to date will plug holes in your practice's defenses.

Wireless Security

Wireless technology has made networking far more convenient. We no longer have to be tethered to ethernet cables wherever we go. This has allowed new devices such as smart TVs and tablets to work anywhere in our homes.

However, wireless networking, WIFI, was not designed with a robust security. The first version of security was known as Wired Equivalent Privacy, WEP. The idea was that it would give the same protection to WIFI networks as being physically plugged into an ethernet cable. It failed miserably and is now considered too insecure to use. Passwords using WEP can be broken in very short time.

The next version of security was called Wi-Fi Protected Access (WPA). It was found to be suspectable to cracking as well and has since been upgraded to WPA2 and then, recently WPA3. WPA2 can be made secure as long as it is configured with a strong password that isn't in a dictionary. More on this a little later.

Why is WIFI so insecure?

If an attacker wanted to break into your ethernet network, they would need to be inside your practice. WIFI transmits well beyond the physical boundaries of your office. With enhanced antennas, an attacker could be hundreds of meters away from your office and still be able to receive the signals. This makes an attack on your wireless network very hard to detect and also prevent.

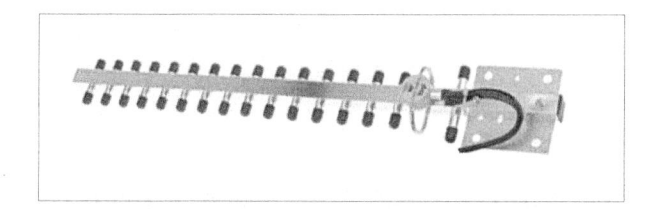

Yagi long range antenna

Hackers have also learned to make their antennas out of different kinds of cans. The first to make headlines was made from a Pringle's tube. But the more effective ones were made from baked beans cans. An antenna made from one of these can receive wireless signals from many hundreds of meters away and cost less than $5 to make. These are called cantennas.

A cantennas made from a baked bean can

WIFI security is all based on several factors but the most important is the encryption. For this, it all comes down to passwords. Attackers can easily break into wireless networks with the same techniques we discussed earlier in the book, dictionary attacks. A basic overview is that the attacker will monitor the WIFI network for a specific kind of traffic. They will be watching for when a new device connects to network and authenticates itself. If no one connects in a reasonable amount of time, the attacker can use a de-authorization attack. This will locate someone who is already connected and send a signal to that device to knock them off the network. The device then will automatically reconnect and when it authenticates, the attacker will capture the traffic. To the user, it will briefly appear that their WIFI was disconnected. Most likely, it will never be noticed.

The attacker will then use that captured traffic and put the authentication session into his password cracker. It will attempt to first go through supplied dictionary files to look for easy passwords. This is where most passwords for WIFI will be cracked. Most people use easy to remember passwords for their WIFI networks.

There are two other elements of WIFI security that some choose to rely on. These are MAC filtering and SSID hiding. Each device that is on a network has a unique MAC address. This is the address of the network adapter at the hardware level. WIFI routers are capable of building a list of approved MAC addresses and then block everyone else. On the surface, this seems like a reasonable way to prevent anyone who isn't authorized from getting onto your network. However, even an attacker with basic wireless cracking skills can easily circumvent this. It is easy to see what MAC addresses are connected. Then the attacker uses software on his computer to change his own MAC to match that of a victim.

The second method, SSID hiding, is where the name of the WIFI network is masked so that only those that are authenticated can see it. Again, this extremely easy for those with basic skills to go around. Neither of these should be considered legitimate security methods to be used on their own.

If they are used in conjunction with a strong WPA2/3 password, then it will add a small level of additional protection. But in the end, wireless security all comes down to the strength of the password.

Your HIPAA Compliant To Do:

Choose a strong password for your WIFI network. WPA2 allows for passwords up to 63 characters long, with a minimum of 8. For the sites we manage, we set 63-character passwords that are completely random. If you don't want to go that far, here are some guidelines for you.

- Set a password that is no less than 15 characters
- Be sure to use upper and lower letters
- Use numbers
- Use punctuation, special characters

One way to do this is to choose 4 or 5 random words and string them together for a passphrase. For example:

Dog table restaurant lawn coffee

That password is 28 characters long. While each word in the password may be in a dictionary, that exact combination won't be. To make things harder, you can add punctuation at the end or beginning. This passphrase would be nearly unbreakable.

Enable MAC filtering as a layer of security for your network. It won't keep out more skilled attackers, but it will help keep out the casual attackers.

If you have a guest network for your patients, make sure it is not on the same network as your practice. It must be completely segregated and have no access to the internal network of your practice.

Set a strong password for the administrator account of your WIFI device. This will keep those that are on your network from gaining access.

Make sure you keep your WIFI up to date with the latest firmware. Each manufacturer releases updates to the firmware of their devices.

Some devices allow you to adjust the transmission strength of the WIFI signals. If you don't have an issue with signal strength, you may want to lower this so that the signals don't travel as far outside your practice.

Consider not allowing employees to use their personal devices on the network. Unless there is a work need for this, there isn't a real need and it opens up a possible vulnerability to your practice's network.

Mobile Device Security

For this section, I will define mobile devices as smartphones, tablets, and laptops.

Mobile devices are becoming more common in medical practices due to how portable they are and the ease of accessing information they provide. Most cloud based EMRs have an app that allows the records to be used on mobile devices. In addition, a significant amount of communication to staff and others has shifted to these mobile devices. Because of that, the access to ePHI on these devices makes them a concern under HIPAA regulations. Laptops may even have ePHI stored on them. Because of this, mobile device security must be addressed in your practice.

The biggest concern for mobile devices is that they will either be lost or stolen. This scenario has led to many breaches.

The Massachusetts Eye and Ear Infirmary and Massachusetts Eye and Ear Associates Inc. (MEEI) reported a laptop stolen to the Office for Civil Rights (OCR) in February 2010. The laptop contained the electronically protected health information (ePHI) of 3,621 individuals on it. The laptop was not encrypted. Data included prescription information as well as clinical information on the patients.

OCR performed an investigation and found that MEEI had failed to comply with specific elements of the HIPAA Security Rule. By reviewing MEEI's Risk Assessment, OCR determined that it wasn't thorough enough to protect ePHI on portable devices. In addition, the policies and procedures in use did not adequately address how to protect ePHI and restrict access to it on any portable device. However, worst of all, OCR found that this behavior had continued for an extended period of time and showed a disregard for HIPAA compliance at MEEI.

OCR fined MEEI $1.5 million and required a corrective action plan be implemented to address the issues that OCR discovered in their investigation. The program would last for 3 years and would require MEEI to make changes in how it protects and restricts access to ePHI.

"In an age when health information is stored and transported on portable devices such as laptops, tablets, and mobile phones, special attention must be paid to safeguarding the information held on these devices. This enforcement action emphasizes that compliance with the HIPAA Privacy and Security Rules must be prioritized by management and implemented throughout an organization, from top to bottom."

--OCR Director Leon Rodriguez

If the device had been encrypted, this would not have been an issue.

The Official HIPAA Jungle Map

Encryption is an addressable requirement under HIPAA regulations.

Addressable requirements give entities discretion on how to handle them, but it doesn't mean that they are optional. They must still be handled in some form. If you determine that encryption isn't needed, be sure to document your reasoning for not using it.

An example is car insurance. The government requires us to carry car insurance if we drive a car. However, it doesn't mandate how we get the insurance or who we purchase it from. Those are left to us to decide and are addressable.

An example of this in healthcare law is the HIPAA Encryption Requirements. You must protect the data but it is up to you to decide the best way to do this. Fortunately, there are free ways to do this for all mobile devices making compliance in this area, very easy.

All smartphones, whether they be Apple or Android, have the ability encrypt the phone. This protects all of the data on the phone itself. However, many Android devices also allow for additional Micro SD memory cards. These must also be encrypted. Android includes a way to do this as well, but it is not the same as the phone encryption.

The next most important item is password policy. A strong password must be used on the device. Numeric only passwords are not secure. Use an alphanumeric password at least 8 characters in length. While facial recognition is the new rage, I would stay away until it has been tested well and shown to be strong. Finger prints are slightly better but have already been broken in some cases.

If your device supports it, enable device wiping after a certain number of incorrect log-in attempts.

Both Apple and Android support remote wiping as well as remote location of devices. Make sure both of these are enabled. This way, you can delete all the data on a lost or stolen device. With remote location, you may be able to track down the device.

For laptops, Microsoft includes BitLocker whole disk encryption in Windows Professional versions. You can use this to encrypt the entire hard drive of the laptop. Then be sure to use a strong password for the laptop. If you choose the option to use the USB key for BitLocker, make sure you don't keep it with the laptop. Otherwise, this will remove the protection of the encryption as the USB key can decrypt the laptop.

Your HIPAA compliance To Do:

Locate any mobile devices that are being used in your practice. This may also include the personal devices of physicians and other staff.

Create policies as to what access these devices will have to ePHI.

Enable device encryption for smartphones and tablets.

Use BitLocker for laptops.

Ensure strong passwords have been used for all devices.

The Official HIPAA Jungle Map

Enable device wiping if too many incorrect passwords have been entered for smartphones and tablets.

Enable remote device wiping for smartphones and tablets

Enable remote device location for smartphones and tablets

Make sure that each device adheres to the policies you created for mobile devices.

BUSINESS ASSOCIATES

HIPAA regulations define a Business Associate as:

A "business associate" is a person or entity that performs certain functions or activities that involve the use or disclosure of protected health information on behalf of, or provides services to, a covered entity. A member of the covered entity's workforce is not a business associate. A covered health care provider, health plan, or health care clearinghouse can be a business associate of another covered entity.

--45 CFR 160.103

In simple terms, if anyone outside of your practice has access to your PHI, then they are a business associate. This means that you need to take steps to ensure that they will protect patient information.

The first step is to talk to the vendor and ask them what steps they have taken to protect PHI in their own business.

The Official HIPAA Jungle Map

Here some questions to ask when you perform your due diligence:

1. When did you perform your last Risk Assessment?
2. What do you do in your practice to protect PHI?
3. Do you have Business Associate Agreements with any parties you outsource to?
4. Do you have anti-malware protection in place on all computers?
5. Do you have a firewall installed?
6. Will you be storing our PHI at your location?
7. How will you backup our PHI?
8. How will you ensure our PHI isn't lost or stolen?
9. Do you use encryption on your mobile devices?
10. How do you physically protect your computers at your office?

While this isn't an exhaustive list of the questions you can ask, it is a very good starting point. This will let you judge the vendor based on their answers. If they state they don't have to do any of these because HIPAA doesn't apply to them, then it's time to start looking for another vendor. If they state that they have never done a Risk Assessment, keep looking.

Once you have found a vendor that is acceptable, have them sign a Business Associate Agreement. One common issue that we hear from practices is that a vendor won't sign the agreement. If they won't, keep looking for another vendor.

Remember, if your vendor is breached, then you will also be held responsible. If you haven't done your due diligence and also obtained a Business Associate Agreement, you will have a hard time showing OCR that you aren't responsible.

Business Associate Agreements are required for any third party that accesses, or has access to your PHI.

Keep copies of all of these Business Associate Agreements in your HIPAA documentation.

Your HIPAA compliance To Do:

Determine what third parties have access to your practice's PHI.

The Official HIPAA Jungle Map

Create a Business Associate Agreement for your practice. You can find an example on HHS's website here:

https://www.hhs.gov/ocr/privacy/hipaa/understanding/coveredentities/contractprov.html

Do you already have Business Associate Agreements with these entities? If not, it's time to get one. If you do, do they need to be updated?

For any entities that you do not yet have a Business Associate Agreement, send a copy of your practice's agreement.

Follow up to make sure that you receive the agreements back.

Keep all of the Business Associate Agreements in your HIPAA documentation.

The Official HIPAA Jungle Map

TRAINING

Under HIPAA regulations, training for your office staff is mandatory. This can be found in two places: as an Administrative Requirement of the HIPAA Privacy Rule (45 CFR §164.530) and an Administrative Safeguard of the HIPAA Security Rule (45 CFR §164.308).

The one specific guideline given for both Covered Entities and Business Associates is:

"implement a security awareness and training program for all members of the workforce"

The guidelines specify a program for training all members of your practice's workforce. This would indicate it's not a single event and rather, is an ongoing system. Security threats to your PHI are always changing.

Five years ago, we didn't have the threat of ransomware, but now it is a very real threat to practices. Phishing has now emerged as one of the greatest threats to the security if PHI.

The Official HIPAA Jungle Map

Has your staff been specifically trained on how to spot a phishing email attack?

The basic HIPAA violations such as throwing away data improperly, leaving a message on the wrong voicemail, and leaving computers unlocked when not attended will never change. Your training program will not need to be updated for those. However, handling phishing, ransomware, and other more sophisticated attacks will need to be updated as the threat evolves.

Training should also be refreshed throughout the year. This is known as security awareness training. Due to the day to day work staff perform, they likely won't remember how to spot a phishing email a few months after training. It's important to keep staff refreshed so that they training will help them protect your practice's PHI.

Recently HHS came up with a standard for the quality of an entity's attempt at HIPAA compliance. It is not focused on training specifically, but it does address training.

Rating	Description
1	The audit results indicate the entity is in compliance with both goals and objectives of the selected standards and implementation specifications.
2	The audit results indicate that the entity substantially meets criteria; it maintains appropriate policies and procedures, and documentation and other evidence of implementation meet requirements.
3	Audit results indicate entity efforts minimally address audited requirements; analysis indicates that entity has made attempts to comply, but the implementation is inadequate, or some efforts indicate a misunderstanding of requirements.
4	Audit results indicate the entity made negligible efforts to comply with the audited requirements – e.g. policies and procedures submitted for review are copied directly from an association template; evidence of training is poorly documented and generic.
5	The entity did not provide OCR with evidence of serious attempt to comply with the Rules and enable individual rights with regard to PHI.

Please notice rating 4.

"Evidence of training is poorly documented and generic. "

This means that standardized training isn't acceptable for compliance. Standardized training would be those that simply go over the most basic of HIPAA violations and don't consider the changing threat environment. A lot of DVD systems would fall into this category since they likely aren't been updated often. Having staff sit down and watch the same DVD won't provide the training they need and now, won't be seen as quality training

Consider having your employees sign off each time they are trained. Some breach investigations found employees claiming that they had never been trained on the entity's policies and procedures. Having your employees sign off will protect you from this.

Your HIPAA compliance To Do:

Take your Risk Assessment and identify the areas where your staff is likely to be exposed to threats.

Build a training outline that addresses these threats.

Create, or purchase, training materials that cover the topics in your outline. Remember, the more interactive the training, the higher the chance your staff will retain the information.

Create a training calendar to ensure that all staff have been trained.

Document the training. Be specific as to who was trained, when, what topics were discussed, and what methods of training were used.

Use your training schedule to have follow up training throughout the year to help staff retain the information. In addition, include any new threats to improper exposure of PHI that may have occurred since your last training.

Have employees sign off that they were trained each time you perform training.

DOCUMENTATION

Where HIPAA regulations are concerned, if it's not documented, it didn't happen. Your documentation is your proof of compliance in the event of an audit. The more information you can provide, the better off you will be. I can't stress this enough, documentation is critical.

Documentation should start with your Risk Assessment. This will identify all of the areas where PHI could be exposed and what you did to address them. It should also cover how you plan to recover from a natural disaster, burglary, or breach.

Keep a copy of each assessment that you do. When you remediate the findings, document those as well and perform a second assessment to show that the discovered issues were addressed.

Using your Risk Assessment, create your practice's policies and procedures. This will address how your practice will protect the privacy of the PHI you possess. Policies and procedures should include the following:

- Patient confidentiality forms
- Confidential communications requests
- How your practice will handle disclosures
- How will your practice handle leaving messages?
- How PHI will be used within the practice
- How PHI will be used by third parties (Business Associates)
- Patient intake process and forms
- Social Media posting, reviews, etc.
- Who has access to your practice's PHI? A current listing of employees
- Email usage
- Computer usage
- Network security configuration
- Workstation and server security
- Mobile device usage
- Employee personal mobile device usage

- Backup and disaster recovery plan
- Breach procedures
- Training
- Audit of access to PHI
- Encryption usage
- Record retention
- Physical security of office

If we refer to the quality of compliance graphic in the previous section, we see that rating 4 states that:

"policies and procedures submitted for review are copied directly from and association template"

HHS is looking to see that you made policies and procedures that are specific to your practice and your circumstances. They don't want to see that you used a generic template. This is why templates for download online are usually not a good idea.

Your Risk Assessment should be able to address most of the issues listed above.

Any time you perform training according to your training program, document it. Be sure to include who was trained, what they were trained on, and how they were trained. Ideally, you would want the employee to also sign off that they were trained. This will protect you from employees stating they were never trained on HIPAA procedures for your practice.

Keeping all Documentation

It's important to keep all of your documentation together in one place. A common mistake practices make is to throw away old documentation that has changed. For example, a Risk Assessment. Keep all of your Risk Assessments each time you do one. It's important to show your compliance over time. One of the items identified in audit settlements is that an entity didn't perform a Risk Assessment for a period of years. It's very important to show that one was done for each year, or whenever something changed in the environment.

Often practices think that when policy has been updated, the old one is no longer needed. This is not the case. It's important to show that you had policies and procedures in place over time.

Be sure you are doing what you state in your documentation

Another mistake entities make is not following their own policies and procedures. The documentation may have everything covered well, but the reality is that those are not being followed in the practice. This can be a huge and costly mistake. First, it means that patient data isn't being protected as it should be. An entity is stating that they are doing their part but not actually following through. Second, it could be viewed as fraudulent activity. It might appear that the documentation was created for the purpose of appearances only and not for the protection of patient data.

Notice of Privacy Practices (NPP)

Each practice is required to have a Notice of Privacy Practices. This document outlines why you collect PHI, how you use it, and also how you will protect the patient's data.

You will need to create one for your practice. Once you have one, each patient should sign one before services are rendered. This should be kept in their chart. In addition, it should be posted in the practice in a place where patients can review it. Lastly, if you have a website, it must be posted there as well.

Patient access to records

Patients have a right to request their records. Practices are required to provide these records in a timely manner in a format requested by a patient. If a cost is involved, patients must be informed of this. The cost should just be for your own costs in relation to this.

Create a policy for your practice that addresses how you will handle these requests.

Ensure that your staff is aware of how these requests should be handled.

In 2019, HHS announced it will start auditing Covered Entities based on complaints by patients who cannot get their records. This will open a lot of practices up to a higher risk of audit.

Be organized

Keep all of your documentation together in one place. This can be a 3-ring binder (or multiple ones if your practice is large enough) or an online service that stores documentation. Make it easy on yourself to keep up with things and maintain your documentation. Also, in the event of an audit, you will be ready to provide the auditor with everything they need if it's all organized. It will make the process much smoother for both of you.

Your HIPAA Compliant To Do:

Use your Risk Assessment to create your policies and procedures.

The Official HIPAA Jungle Map

Save all documentation in one central area, a 3-ring binder or online.

Be sure that you are actually doing what your policies and procedures state. Many sites have been fined for not actually following through on their own policies stated and it resulted in a breach.

Create your NPP and make sure each patient reviews and signs it. Also make sure it is posted in your practice and online if you have a website for your practice.

As you have more documentation, new employee hires, terminations, employee trainings, etc., put it into your HIPAA documentation.

Each year when you perform a Risk Assessment, add it to your documentation. Keep all previous copies as well.

Remember, if it's not documented, it didn't happen.

HIPAA COMPLIANCE ROAD MAP

This section is a guide that covers all of the topics discussed in this book in an outline format. While it is not all inclusive and every part won't fit for every single practice, it is a guide for you to create your practice's compliance program.

Following the items in this outline will put you far ahead in compliance and will help you to be able to protect your practice from most breaches. It will also help you to prepare in the event you ever do find yourself audited.

Designate key staff members

- Who is the Privacy Officer?
- Who is the Security Officer?
- Will any other staff members need to be involved?

Perform a HIPAA Risk Assessment

- Perform a physical audit of your site

- Create an asset list of all computers and devices on your network
- Document all areas, or gaps, that need to be addressed

Place a copy of this initial assessment with your HIPAA documentation

- This will prove that you have identified your vulnerabilities

DON'T STOP HERE! Continue by resolving any issues your Risk Assessment discovered.

Create a remediation plan to address all of the gaps you have identified

- Document your plan in writing and add it to your HIPAA documentation

Execute your remediation plan

- Document the steps you took to address the gaps you found

- Place this documentation with your HIPAA documentation

Encryption of certain assets

- Did your Risk Assessment identify mobile devices or backup systems that will require encryption?
- If so, have you encrypted these devices?
- Ensure that your policies and procedures indicate what devices you have encrypted

Perform a second Risk Assessment that shows all gaps have been addressed

- If gaps cannot be addressed, notate that in your documentation
- Place this second Risk Assessment into your HIPAA documentation
- For each new assessment you are required to do, add it to your documentation

Create your notice of Privacy Practices

- Ensure each patient signs your notice

The Official HIPAA Jungle Map

- Have you put your notice on your website?
- Is your notice posted in your office?

Create your training program

- Identify the areas you will train on
- Decide on the method you will use to train (online, DVDs, live in person)
- Create a training calendar for your yearly HIPAA training
- Ensure all staff, including physicians, have undergone HIPAA training
- Perform periodic security awareness training that updates staff on new threats to PHI
- Have each employee sign off that they have been trained after each training session (who was trained, what they trained on, how they were trained, when they are trained)

Create your network and computer security policy

- Do you have a business level firewall?

The Official HIPAA Jungle Map

- Is someone monitoring the firewall logs? How often?
- Are all of your computers using supported operating systems?
- Are your computers being monitored for new patches? Are these being installed? How often?
- Does each computer have anti-malware software that allows for real time monitoring?
- Are computer event logs being monitored? How often?
- Are you monitoring for unapproved programs being installed on your computers?
- What is your password policy?
- Are you using Lastpass for your online passwords?
- Is your office WIFI using a strong password for its encryption?
- Is your guest WIFI on the same network as your office?

The Official HIPAA Jungle Map

Create a policy for communications outside the practice

- If you use email to communicate with patients, is it encrypted?
- If you use SMS, ensure it is a secure service

Create your monitoring of PHI access policy

- Are you monitoring your EMR logs to ensure that staff aren't accessing PHI they have no need to access?
- Are you monitoring your server's security log to ensure staff aren't accessing files they don't need to?
- Are you monitoring that former employees aren't accessing records?
- Are you monitoring any VPN access?

Create your disaster and recovery policy

- Identify the data, including PHI, that you will need to back up
- What method will you use to back up the data?
- How will you recover from a ransomware attack?

The Official HIPAA Jungle Map

- How will you recover from an office theft?
- How will you recover from a natural disaster?
- Are you using cloud storage? Do you have a Business Associate Agreement?

Gather Business Associate Agreements for all necessary third parties

- Create your practice's Business Associate Agreement
- Send agreement to all third parties who have access to your PHI
- Ensure that you get one back for each vendor
- Put all agreements into your HIPAA documentation

Create your Breach Notification policy

- Who is the point person in your practice for a breach?
- Who needs to be contacted to assist in the breach?
- Who is responsible for reporting to HHS, patients, and the media?

Create your records disposal policy

The Official HIPAA Jungle Map

- If you have paper records, how will you securely dispose of them?
- How will you dispose of old computers or devices?

Create your patient access to records policy

- When patients request their records, are you providing the records to them?
- What format will you provide these records in?
- What is your policy for time required to deliver and are there fees involved?

Create your policies and procedures

- Take all the polices you created above and put them into one documented place
- Create any additional polices that your practice needs such as computer usage, social media

CONCLUSION

HIPAA regulations can be very confusing for practices. This is especially true for smaller practices that may not have the manpower or budget to learn the things that are required. Unfortunately, this doesn't relieve them of the responsibility of these regulations.

This book's purpose was to help give you a road map to start your HIPAA compliance. You can't ignore it and the chances of having a breach are increasing every day.

Why take that chance?

Follow the steps outlined in this book and you will be much further along than you were before. This book covers the majority of the items you need to address. HHS is looking to see if you take hap seriously and are doing your part to protect patient data. Deciding that you can't afford it or don't have time to address it isn't going to go over well.

HHS has shown their willingness to increase the number of audits and the amounts of fines year after year. Don't let your practice end up on the HIPAA Wall of Shame.

Get More Information at Our Blog

This book is the product of our blog, Your HIPAA Guide. Over the last 10 years, I have noticed a significant amount of misunderstanding and misinformation concerning HIPAA and compliance within the medical community. I first started to write our blog as a way to help get better information out to those who needed it. Over time, this morphed into training courses and then this book.

People consume information in different ways. Some want to read a book, some want to watch videos, and some are fine with shorter blog posts. My goal has been to get the information to those who need it in a format that works best for them.

The Official HIPAA Jungle Map

HIPAA isn't going away. In fact, given the increase in the focus of cybersecurity, HIPAA will become even more obvious as time goes on.

The blog we created is updated often with information targeted to the small practice. It is actionable and will help you know just what you need to do.

You can find it at:

http://www.yourhipaaguide.com/

Thank you for reading and I hope this has been of some small service to you.

Todd Dixon

Iron Comet Consulting, Inc.

ABOUT THE AUTHOR

Todd Dixon is the owner of Iron Comet Consulting, Inc., a cybersecurity and compliance firm in the Atlanta area of Georgia. He has worked with the unique needs of medical practices and their IT for over 20 years.

He has achieved the following certifications:

CompTIA CASP+

CompTIA CySA+

CompTIA Pentest+

CompTIA Security+

(ISC)² HCISPP

Todd specializes in working with small to mid-sized practices to help them secure their networks and achieve HIPAA compliance.

If you need help with your HIPAA compliance or just have questions, we can help.

The Official HIPAA Jungle Map

You can reach us at:

Iron Comet Consulting, Inc.

770-506-4383

www.IronComet.com

We have been serving the unique IT needs of medical practices for more than 20 years. We have the expertise you need to solve your IT, security, and compliance issues.

Made in the USA
Middletown, DE
11 July 2025